10/20

bee fearless

bee fearless

Dream like a Kid

Mikaila ULMER

with **Brin Stevens**

putnam

G. P. PUTNAM'S SONS

G. P. PUTNAM'S SONS

An imprint of Penguin Random House LLC, New York

Copyright © 2020 by Mikaila Ulmer

G. P. Putnam's Sons is a registered trademark of Penguin Random House LLC.

Visit us online at penguinrandomhouse.com

Library of Congress Cataloging-in-Publication Data is available.

Printed in the United States of America
ISBN 9781984815088

1 3 5 7 9 10 8 6 4 2

Design by Ryan Thomann
Text set in Aleo
Lemon icons and honeycomb pattern courtesy of Shutterstock.
Photographs reprinted with permission of the Ulmer family.

This book is dedicated to all the bee-lievers,
people young and old who dream like kids
and create their own paths to success.

ing.
g.

Love to
LEMONADE

bee
change

save
bees

Pollen.
Nation.

bee
curious

Gimme a
hive five!

th
se

let's make
this house
a 'comb

bees

It always seems impossible until it's done.

-*Nelson Mandela*

Introduction

When I was
four and a half years old, I got
my first bee sting. *Ouch!* I don't know if
you've ever been stung by a bee, but it hurts. My parents
put a little aloe on it, and the pain eventually went away.
Then, a week later, I got stung again! I didn't know what
was going on, but I decided I was never going outside again,
because I was afraid if I did, I'd get stung by another bee.
My parents said, "You can't stay inside forever." Instead of
fearing the bees, my parents encouraged me to find out
more about them and why they sting. I learned that bees
sting when they're scared, and they're trying to protect
themselves against big creatures like four-year-old girls.
But I learned something else—more than just about bee

stings. The bees were in trouble: They were disappearing at an alarming rate, and they needed our help. I didn't quite understand the full story at that age, but I decided to set up a lemonade stand outside my house to raise money to protect the bees. I got a little creative and decided to sweeten my lemonade with honey, since bees make honey.

Within a few years, I was bottling my lemonade and selling it in a few stores in Austin, Texas, where I live. A few more years later, my lemonade stand, along with my mission to save the bees, had grown into a multimillion-dollar social enterprise. Now my lemonade is available nationwide in over 1,500 stores. Since starting my company in 2009, I've sold over 1.2 million bottles of lemonade. In that time, I have saved an estimated 800,000 bees, with a target of saving an additional 400,000 bees by the end of 2020. That's a lot of happy bees!

I want to share with you my story of how my simple lemonade stand grew into a successful national business.

This book is about more than just how I built a lemonade company and why you should save the bees. It's about how to gain the confidence to build a business from the ground up, to take on a problem in our society, to get in front of people and advocate for what you believe in. To be charitable in action, not just talk. It's about how to be a beautifully mindful entrepreneur.

I've learned the things that make a great entrepreneur are qualities that come naturally to kids. We dream big. We don't see obstacles, but we do see opportunity. We dream about things that don't even exist yet. And we believe in the future. Kids are quite possibly the biggest dreamers of all. We jump out of bed in the morning and have the wildest ideas. We grab our notebooks, write them down, and figure out how to make them real. If you come up with a good idea and work hard, you can be successful. That's what our parents tell us. That's what our teachers tell us. And so that's what we tell ourselves.

We believe in the impossible. We see possibilities where adults see problems. Like a lot of dreams, I didn't see mine coming. I didn't have any experience running a beverage company; neither did my parents or my two brothers—my older brother, Khalil, and my younger brother, Jacob. But I did know that I wanted to protect the bees from going extinct through my lemonade stand, and I was going to make it happen.

Here's where it gets a little scary: How do you learn to run a business? It's not just talking about passion and creativity and dreams. It's about real things like the markets and banks, buyers and sellers, investors and debt, marketing and branding—in other words, there's a whole lot more to running a business than I ever thought. And it gets even scarier. It's also about making really big decisions and taking risks.

But here's where it's not scary: If you say to yourself, *How hard is it to start a business?* Your answer should always be, *Starting a business is not hard when you're having fun.* Then ask, *Why am I starting a business?* Your answer should be, *Because I believe it will make the world better.* So why not start now?

My goal for this book is to show you how. I truly believe there is no age restriction for who can impact the world in positive ways. Even kids can solve all sorts of very big problems. And with the power of technology that generations before us invented, our generation and future generations have more opportunities than ever to research, learn, connect, and spread our messages and our missions around the world.

When you're having fun, learning something new, and doing something for the right reasons, you're being creative and meeting people and putting your energy to good use. Nothing can stop you when you're doing something you love.

So why am I, a fifteen-year-old girl from Austin, Texas, writing a book about business? Because I know that if we all go out in this world looking together at the possibilities of things rather than just the problems, our future will be a whole lot brighter by the time we're the average age of a CEO.

So...

Let's b🐝gin!

---Mikaila

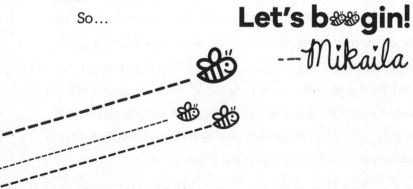

CHAPTER ONE

Bee Stings

A lot of people
ask me how I started my business.
Did you just decide to set up a lemonade stand? The
answer is yes, I did just decide to set up a lemonade stand,
but a lot of steps came before that.

It all started in a faraway land called Austin, Texas.
At just four years old, while I was touring my soon-to-be
kindergarten at Trinity Episcopal School, one of the teachers
was showing me various classrooms at the elementary and
middle school, and I remember thinking everything felt so
big and new and shiny compared to my preschool, which
was a small, dated building with only a couple classrooms.
On one of the benches outside the library sat a colorful
flyer advertising a business fair.

"Hey, what's that say?" I said to my mom. I was always asking my parents questions.

She looked at the flyer and casually said, "That's something called Acton Children's Business Fair."

"That sounds fun. I like fairs," I said with a smile.

"Would you want to sign up for that?" my mom asked with a little more interest. The only requirement was that I had to be at least four years old. I was four and a half years old, so I qualified.

I said, "Yes, Mommy, I want to do that!" Then I paused and thought about it. "What's a business fair?" I knew what a fair was, but I didn't really know what they meant by *business*. "Will there be rides and games?"

"No, probably not." She laughed. "It's a different kind of fair." She explained in basic terms what a business was and how the fair might be organized.

"So I would sell something at the fair?" I kind of understood.

"Yes," she said.

"Okay! Let's sign up."

When we got home from the school tour that day, my mom and I registered online for the fair. And she wrote the date of the fair on the family calendar in big red ink. The one rule about the family calendar is that when it goes up, we can't forget about it. Although we did have enough time to forget about it, since it was five months away, in September, it still felt like not enough time to figure out what I was going to sell.

I decided that over the summer I would test out some business ideas. One day I thought I would create something fun and pretty for people to buy, so I searched for flowers in our garden and then took Play-Doh, rolled them into balls with the flowers, and tried to sell them. After grabbing my little craft table and chair from my room, I sat and waited on my front lawn for customers. As you can imagine, it didn't go very well, but I did learn that in order to sell your product, it needs to be a product that people want to buy. So I thought about selling my drawings, or even making bracelets. Everyone likes to buy bracelets—maybe people would buy my product! I was getting somewhere. Everywhere I went, I came up with ideas of new things to sell. Slime with glitter, painted rocks, lip balm that maybe my parents would let me wear (because I wasn't allowed to wear lip gloss or lipstick yet).

I would continue to test out new ideas and figure out exactly what I was going to sell.

This is where the bees came in.

I don't remember much about being stung by my first bee, because I was only four and a half years old, but I do remember one part clearly. I got stung in the neck. The neck! I was at a neighbor's party up the hill from our house when it happened. Friends were there, and they were playing music. I was spinning around, dancing with my arms stretched out when something hit my face, so I went to swat at it, and I clearly remember hitting something with my hand. I must have made the bee angry, because before I knew it, something sharp hit my neck. My family was there, and there was lots of crying. After a while, my neck stopped burning and started to sting. I guess that's why they call it a bee *sting*. All around our neighborhood were large aloe plants. My dad tore off a piece of an aloe leaf and told me to hold it to my neck. I did as he instructed, and sulked for the rest of the party.

Then, exactly one week later, when we were at a family cookout, I got my second bee sting. This time in my ear! Two different bees, two different places. I actually thought that I would now get stung every time I went outside, or at least every seven days.

After the second bee sting, I didn't even want to go outside, not even to help my dad in our garden or play with my little brother, Jacob. I tried to avoid any interaction with a bee and didn't want to go near anything with wings. This was a problem for my family. We're very outdoorsy, and not leaving the house wasn't an option. My parents sat me down one evening and said, "Mikaila, you can choose to be afraid of bees. But that would mean not going outside and enjoying all the things you love to do. Or, instead of being afraid of bees, you could learn about them." So we went to the library, and my bee research began.

Twin Oaks Branch Library was just a few blocks from my home, and I loved visiting it because it was always quiet and cool. In Austin, where our winters could be just as hot as our summers, you were always looking for places to escape the heat.

When I was a little girl, my favorite day of the week was Monday. Every Monday, my mom would take me to the library. I don't remember our walks to and from the library, but my mom tells me I would stop every few steps to inspect something new: "Look, what's that?" A few more steps. "And what's that?" I was always asking questions. It took us a very long time to go a short distance.

When we got to the library, I had just as many questions about things. The library was a place where I could get a lot of answers to a lot of questions. I thought that was awesome! "The library knows everything!" I would say. I learned how to read when I was very young. My parents were amazed at how quickly I picked up words. I read to know the answers to my questions.

I always wanted to check out as many books as I could, but the librarian reminded me there was a limit. And my mom would remind me there were only so many books we could carry home. I had to decide which ones to choose, and it was always difficult. In my mind, there were so many topics to explore: from outer space to the deepest oceans. These books took me to unimaginable places. By Tuesday, I was ready for more books.

But the day I went to the library after I had been stung by two bees, I knew exactly what I was looking for: bee books.

At four-and-a-half, I couldn't read most of the complicated subjects, but there were a few picture books in the
kids' section, so I started with those. I tried to learn anything and everything about bees! I also checked out a video
about bee pollination. I remember the video played that
wild *Flight of the Bumblebee* music by Nikolai Rimsky-
Korsakov. My mom explained the music was from an opera
and was well known. I buzzed around the living room like
a bee in an opera. I thought it was fascinating that the video
was told from the perspective of the bee, who said things
like *I'm super fuzzy, and pollen sticks to the hair on my legs
when I visit flowers.* The bees then move the pollen to a special area on their back legs called pollen baskets. That was
interesting. I didn't know that. I stopped buzzing around the
room and really paid attention. *Without me, you wouldn't
be able to eat most fruits, nuts, cheeses, or any dairy, because
cows eat alfalfa and alfalfa is pollinated by bees.*

"Is this true?" I asked my parents with wide eyes.

"Yes, it's true," they said.

"Isn't ice cream dairy?"

"Yes."

"So no ice cream?"

No ice cream.

Even though I wasn't able to fully grasp the effect of bees
on our environment, I still realized many things I loved to
eat, not just honey, came from bees. Yes, they stung, and
yes, they were a little scary for that reason, but they were
an important part of our world. I also learned that bees

were dying at an alarming rate. So I decided I was going to save them. But how?

Without knowing it, I was doing the first three most important steps in starting a business: First, I was identifying a problem; second, I was researching the problem; and finally, I was starting to do something I felt passionate about. These first three steps are critical. You always want to clearly identify and research your problem before you get started, and you always want to be involved in a business or product you're passionate about. I can't stress this enough. If you are not passionate about your idea, it will be hard to stay engaged in the work it takes to grow a business. And believe me, there's a lot of work ahead of you when you start a business.

Buzziness

IDEA

The first three steps in starting a business:

1
IDENTIFYING
A PROBLEM

2
RESEARCHING
THE PROBLEM

3
DOING
SOMETHING YOU
FEEL PASSIONATE
ABOUT

I had continued to test out ideas for the business fair, but nothing was really exciting me. Then, two months after my first bee sting and one month after touring the school, my family and I were driving around Austin running errands and we saw lemonade stands on street after street. At first we thought all the kids serving lemonade must be a coincidence—it was a really hot day, after all. But we soon learned there was something called Austin Lemonade Day, where kids set up lemonade stands to help earn money for different causes.

Turns out Lemonade Day is an event that happens every May. It was launched in 2007 in Houston, Texas, to teach kids how to start and run their own businesses. Since then, it has expanded to include more than a million child participants in the United States and Canada.

Of course I insisted on stopping at every stand we passed. I saw how much fun all the kids were having learning how to handle and count money, serve customers, and support a cause they loved! One child we met was raising money for a food pantry, another for sea turtles, another for a family trip. There were so many fun lemonade stands, and so many kids, and so many good causes!

I wanted to go home immediately and set up my own lemonade stand and start helping the bees. But it was getting late, and I had already missed Lemonade Day. Our house is near a church, so I could certainly set up and sell lemonade the next day, which was a Sunday, and donate to the bees.

The next morning, I woke up early to the sound of

church bells and got to work in the kitchen. *I can make my own Lemonade Day,* I thought. We had some lemons and plenty of sugar, but I decided to replace the sugar with honey, since my mission was to save the bees. I would set up a lemonade stand in front of my house using my craft table and chair, and sell to the churchgoers as they left. I took a pitcher, drizzled in tons of honey, squeezed a couple lemons, then added water. I had made my first official batch of lemonade!

And it was *awful.*

When I tasted it, my face bunched up from the sourness.

When my mother tasted it, she agreed. We poured it down the drain and started over. It was a little better the next time, but I could tell she was upset that the kitchen was a mess and that I'd wasted lots of ingredients. There were pitchers everywhere, sticky sugar on the countertops, honey on the floor, and lots of cups on the table.

I got to work designing a poster.

"How much should I sell my lemonade for?" I asked my dad.

"What seems like a fair price?" he responded.

I didn't know anything about the cost of things but remembered most kids on Lemonade Day were selling their lemonade for a dollar, so I decided I'd sell mine for the same price.

"That seems reasonable," he said.

The poster said DRINK LEMONADE AND SAVE THE BEES! Then below, it read $1.00. SMILES FREE!! I brought out the lemonade, then I waited for people to show up.

It didn't take long before an older couple stood in front of my table. They talked about the sun being hot and they were very thirsty. Suddenly, I got really nervous and shy, so I ran and hid behind my lemonade pitcher. I had tried to sell a few painted rocks to my neighbors, but they were people I knew. Selling lemonade to strangers was different and suddenly scary because I didn't know what to say or what they'd say back to me. My parents told me I needed to be polite and introduce myself, then introduce my product. Then they said to talk about the bees. I did the best I could. When the couple left, my parents told me to be confident in myself. It took a few more tries to shake off the jitters. After a few more customers, I was calling to people on the street, "Buy my lemonade and save the bees!" Then I'd talk about my lemonade and tell people how important the bees are to our planet. I even made some money—fifteen dollars, to be exact, which felt like a whole lot to a four-and-a-half-year-old! We still have the first dollar I made at that lemonade stand mounted in a frame in our house.

That night, my parents asked if I had a bee organization in mind that I planned to donate the money to.

I said, "Yes, I know exactly which one, but first I want to buy a doll." I had been eyeing this beautiful doll my cousin got for Christmas, and I wanted it more than anything, and then I'd give the rest to a bee foundation.

"Oh," my mom said with a little chuckle. "But you told your customers you were raising money to save the bees."

"I am!" I said defensively. "But I also want a doll."

"You only earned a small amount of money," my mom said. "The doll you are interested in buying is much more than fifteen dollars."

I was very surprised by this. I had been out selling lemonade in the hot sun for almost an hour—to a kid, an hour is an eternity—and even though I didn't get a ton of customers, some people had given me extra money as a tip. I thought I had done a great job and made a lot of money, considering I only had a morning to prepare.

"You don't have enough for both a donation and a doll, so what do you think you should do?" my dad asked.

This made me think of something my father told me my great-grandpa Jake always said to him and his brother. He never thought of himself as an entrepreneur, even though he ran a small but successful house-painting business. He would say, "You gotta give before you get." Give first, save next, spend later. That was his secret. Think about others first, think about your future next, and enjoy the benefits of hard work later.

"Give, save, spend, like Grandpa Jake always said," I replied to my father.

"Exactly," my dad said with a smile.

This would also become integral to my mission as I grew my business, and it is important when considering how you create and manage your own company. Always, no matter

Buzziness IDEA

Consider three practices as you grow your business: GIVE, SAVE, SPEND, in that order.

Create a mindset around charity because it is much more rewarding to sell a product that has a mission.

Save because it's forward-thinking about your financial security.

Finally, spend because you should be able to enjoy your hard work.

what, always begin with giving—and giving can be done for free if you're giving time and energy toward something. So it's important to consider all three practices of give, save, spend, in that order: give first, save next, spend later. You have to create a mindset around charity, and here is why: As you move forward in building your company, you will realize that giving is the most important lesson because making someone else happy feels good. It's one thing to sell a product, but it's another thing, and a much more rewarding pursuit, to sell a product that has a mission behind it—like protecting the bees—and gives back to the world at the same time. Saving comes next because it's forward-thinking about the financial security of you and your company, and you'll need to save in order to grow your business. Always be thinking of your next step. And finally, spending is important because you should be able to enjoy your hard work. Just don't make spending your priority. My parents say not only is the practice of giving, saving, and spending important in business but also an important way to live your life in general. Give before you get!

"Do you know what bee nonprofit you would like to donate your money to?" my mom asked again.

I knew the exact organization, but I couldn't remember its name.

"I want to give to the one where you can buy farm animals and donate them to a family. That's what I want to do, but with bees," I told my parents. They knew right away I was referring to Heifer International. We went online to donate my fifteen dollars, but when we went to donate a hive of bees, it cost thirty dollars.

"I didn't raise enough for the donation I want!" I said with surprise.

"Every little bit matters, and I'm sure you could find another organization that would take your fifteen dollars," my mom said.

"Or," I said, my mind racing with ideas, "I could use the money I made to have another lemonade stand and raise even *more* money for the bees." I only needed a few dollars to buy a couple lemons and more sugar. I had enough cups, and water was pretty much free, in my mind.

"That way I could donate a whole hive of bees—or two—through Heifer International, save to grow my business, and later buy my doll!" I had the solution.

"If you are serious about selling lemonade, getting a doll, *and* saving the bees, you need a good recipe," my dad said nicely.

I guess I hadn't noticed, but my batch of honey lemonade had made more than a few customers wince.

The next day, my parents said they were taking me on an important trip. I was very excited. I loved surprise trips. When they pulled into our bank's parking lot, I thought they were running an errand first.

"We're here!" my dad announced.

"I thought you were taking me someplace special," I said.

"Banks are special," he said.

"Why?" I was genuinely confused.

"A bank is a special place where people keep their money."

"I already have a place where I keep my money, in my piggybank."

My parents chuckled.

"Banks are places where you can keep more money," my dad explained.

My uncle Alphonso had given me a check for fifty dollars on my fourth birthday, which my father took out of an envelope, plus I had the fifteen dollars I had made from my lemonade stand.

"You're going to open your own savings account."

A **savings account** is a place where you can safely keep your money and withdraw money when you need it.

I had gone to this bank many times before with my parents. I liked the bank because they had a jar of lollipops on a table, and stickers.

My mom handed me a deposit slip and taught me where to fill in the numbers: "Fifty from Uncle Alphonso, plus the fifteen you made selling lemonade."

They're always trying to tie in math, spelling, and reading lessons to everyday activities, which is pretty creative.

I started to write in the information, but my mother stopped me.

"You need to write your name and numbers more neatly or the teller might not read the information accurately."

So I started over, concentrating hard on writing my numbers to make sure each one was as clearly written down as possible. Then I signed my name on the back of Uncle Alphonso's check, as my parents instructed. I remember my signature looked sloppy compared to how my mother beautifully signed her checks.

"I've had many more years of practice signing my name." She winked. "You'll get there."

Next, they told me I had to go see the teller.

"The teller? What is she going to tell me?"

My parents laughed.

"The teller is an employee of the bank who is trained to handle your money. She will take your money and deposit it into an account, and she can withdraw money from your account for you as well."

"When you speak with the teller, be confident and clear with what you want," my father said.

"Aren't you coming with me?" I asked a little hesitantly.

"No, it's your money, and you can do this on your own," my mother said firmly.

They were reinforcing the lesson that I had a voice and was important, and I could speak for myself. Plus, doing it on my own gave me a lot of confidence. I wanted to be more independent.

The teller was a very nice woman. She took my birthday check, my fifteen dollars cash, and my deposit slip, and ran it through a machine, then I got a slip back with my account's balance. I officially had my first-ever savings account, with sixty-five dollars in it.

So now I had money in a bank account. My goal was to fund-raise for the bees, but I also needed more money to grow my lemonade stand, and I wanted a little extra left to buy a doll.

All I needed now was a better lemonade recipe. I would keep experimenting with ingredients until I got my formula just right.

I didn't know it at the time, but I was doing the next important step to starting a business, after identifying a problem and researching a problem, and that is to come up with a solution to your problem. In my case, the problem I identified and researched was that the bees were dying. The solution was to protect them by finding ways to contribute money to bee conservation causes like donating to organizations that protected the bees or supporting local beekeepers. That meant making really good lemonade that people would want to buy!

CHAPTER TWO

From Stings to Wings

A week later,
a package arrived in the mail.
It was from my great-granny Helen on my
dad's side. She lived in South Carolina and loved to cook.
She was always calling my parents to talk about new recipes. She must have been talking to my parents about my
adventures in the kitchen, because she had sent me a cookbook. It was published in the 1940s and had all these old
recipes in it. Instead of butter, recipes called for oleo (or
margarine) and lard. It had a tattered cover and ink coming
off the pages. The binding was stringy, and between pages
there were other recipes written on pieces of paper. Even
the pages had yellowed over time.

I was thumbing through the cookbook, with help from

my mom. Besides finding recipes that called for ingredients that I'd never heard of, we also found a lemonade recipe that looked interesting. It was a recipe for flaxseed lemonade. Like most of the recipes in the cookbook, my great-grandma had made notes on the page, scratched out certain ingredients, and added new ones to make it her own. The recipe was different from all other lemonade recipes I'd ever seen because it was served hot.

"Hot lemonade?" I asked my dad.

My dad smiled this great big smile as if it had stirred a distant memory.

"Ah, yes. My grandma used to make me this recipe when I got sick."

"Oh! I don't want to make that kind of lemonade. I want to make lemonade for people who are thirsty."

"Well, we could cool it down," my mom suggested.

I thought that sounded like a good idea.

"And what is flaxseed?" I asked my parents.

My mom said, "It helps keep you going." That sounded healthy.

It turns out flaxseed is packed with fiber, antioxidants, and omega-3s, which are great for your body and your brain, and it wasn't in the nut category—I'm allergic to nuts, so this was good news. Flaxseed was also, I would learn later, one of the oldest fiber crops in the world, originally cultivated in ancient Egypt and China, which I thought was pretty neat.

In doing a little more research, I learned the benefits

of honey were just as impressive. Honey is one of the few foods that contains pinocembrin, an antioxidant linked to improving brain functioning.

My mom, who helps market other companies, said flaxseed was an unusual ingredient, plus it was a healthy ingredient, and it might draw more customers to my lemonade stand. My parents are pretty health conscious. My mom had been reading the backs of food labels ever since I could remember. She was always pointing out ingredients, including high fructose corn syrup. It was kind of gross and scary when we started to measure out all the different types of sugar in things. There was a lot of talk about the negative effects of high fructose corn syrup on the body—and it was the second ingredient listed in many lemonades and juices. I didn't want my lemonade to be a negative, I wanted it to be a positive, so the honey seemed to not only promote saving the bees but also be a healthy alternative to other sweeteners.

My mom said I might have found a clever alternative to most of the lemonades being sold in grocery stores. The wheels in my brain started to turn. One of the suggestions of the Acton Children's Business Fair was to create a product that was unique. I had never seen or tasted healthy lemonade with flaxseed or honey in it before. That seemed unique and supported my mission to help the bees.

"Mommy, is flaxseed honey lemonade a unique product?"

She laughed. "Yes, I think it's a unique product. And healthy, too."

"Unique enough for the business fair?"

She thought for a moment and said, "I think it would be!"

I had a problem I wanted to solve, and now I had an idea for solving it: *How do you take a basic idea—such as making lemonade—and make it your own? Maybe I can create a healthier version of lemonade that isn't already being sold.* For others, inspiration might come from something you felt could be made better in this world, like sweaters that aren't itchy, or sandwich bags that aren't made out of plastic. Maybe a medical device that could help save a life. Or let's say one of your family members or a friend has experienced an illness or has a specific problem that needs solving: *If only there were a product out there that could help.* . . . Look around, there are lots of things that need fixing. For me, it started with inspiration from a couple bee stings and my great-grandmother's flaxseed lemonade recipe. The problem was how to save the bees; the solution was creating an unusual, healthy recipe using honey to bring attention to my mission and donate to organizations helping bees. So I would begin with my great-grandmother's recipe. Of course I couldn't use the cookbook recipe, I had to make the recipe my own, so that meant a lot of experimenting with different ingredients and different cooking methods in the kitchen, and a lot of trial and error.

First, with the help of my parents, I made my

great-granny Helen's original cook-book recipe as our test recipe. The flaxseeds needed to be steeped over the stove, then the flaxseed liquid needed to be drained. I was nervous about getting burned; I was still only four and a half years old, and not comfortable around hot things like stoves. The recipe called for sugar to sweeten it, not honey, and it was sup-posed to be served hot. So that was different. I followed the recipe to a T. It was warm and satisfying, but it

Buzziness IDEA

When thinking of a business idea, find a problem you want to solve. Look around—there are lots of things that need fixing, and a lot that can inspire you.

was only the test recipe, the inspiration behind what would eventually become my healthier version of lemonade.

Next, my parents and I tested different ingredients and methods to make it original. I made another batch of great-granny Helen's recipe, but instead of warming it up, I experimented by cooling the ingredients and serving it cold. This made the consistency of the lemonade too thick in an unpleasant way. I discovered flaxseeds thicken only slightly when they're heated but get too thick when they're cooled. Then I made the recipe again, substituting honey for the sugar. It was way too thick and way too sweet—so sweet I could feel the sweetness in my cheeks after only one sip.

So, again, I started over. My arms were starting to get kind of sore. I had a handheld lemon squeezer at that point, so I stood on a chair at the kitchen counter and squeezed lemons by hand—delicious lemonade requires a lot of lemon juice. I was not very tall for my age, so everything I tried to measure and pour I did with little hands, and not yet as carefully as an adult might. It got a bit chaotic.

"Maybe you should create a chart of all the possibilities, listing each ingredient, amount, and method, and write down your thoughts after each batch," my father suggested. So that's exactly what I did. It took a couple weeks to chart each tweak of each recipe. There were dozens of pitchers and various containers in my refrigerator, labeled so that I could keep track: "Recipe 1-A" or "Recipe 2-A" and so on, depending on the ingredients and methods I was using for each recipe. Then I invited friends and family over to taste the different recipes. One neighbor, Mr. Jeff, owned a heating and cooling company and spent a lot of time in people's hot attics—he was one of my best tasters! One day, after tasting half a dozen new recipes, he said, "Never in my life have I had so much lemonade as in these last couple weeks." He wrote down his comments after each test.

I couldn't have come up with my final recipe without my wonderful taste testers. I would receive comments from them like "I can *really* taste the honey in this one..." or "Wow, too sour. Maybe fewer lemons."

Once I got a good sense of the final recipe, we added a few other ingredients, such as fresh mint from our garden, and when everyone had cast their vote, we finally had our winning recipe! It was unique and healthy *and* delicious.

Now that I had my own original lemonade recipe, I had to determine a few other things to feel prepared for the Acton Children's Business Fair. My parents had given some simple tips on how to buy supplies and sell my product. The fair also had a guide called "3 Magic Seeds: Discovering the Entrepreneurial Spirit." It advised that an aspiring child entrepreneur should:

1. Make something with his or her own hands.
2. Sell it (safely) to a stranger.
3. Experience the freedom (and responsibility) of having a little extra spending money as a reward.

I had followed the 3 Magic Seeds: I had made lemonade with my hands; I had sold it to strangers; and I had made a little money.

But there was something missing. Something important.

"Have you thought of a name for your business?" my dad asked.

Business? I hadn't thought of my lemonade stand as a business. But I had thought of a name.

"Yes. I'm going to call my company BeeSweet Lemonade!" I said proudly.

I had been thinking of names for a while. It was the only name I loved, and it stuck in my head, so that was it.

"*B-e* Sweet or *B-e-e* Sweet?" My father already knew the answer, but he was always trying to find ways to get me to spell words.

"Both! Be Sweet and BeeSweet. But we'll spell it *B-E-E* Sweet!" I said with a giggle.

I had two reasons for naming my business BeeSweet. First, because my lemonade was sweetened with honey, which the bees made, and second, because I wanted people to be sweet and help save the bees with me.

My first business fair

❀ ❀ ❀

The Acton Children's Business Fair was created by a couple named Jeff and Laura Sandefer in Austin in 2007. They wanted to encourage kids to learn about entrepreneurship. An **entrepreneur** is someone who organizes and starts a business, usually doing so with financial risk involved.

Austin is known for its entrepreneurs. Dell Computers started here in
Austin; so did Kendra Scott jewelry
and Sweet Leaf Tea. Blake Mycoskie,
the founder of TOMS Shoes, went
to my high school (many years earlier!). Entrepreneurship runs in the
heart of this city, and the business
fair was an opportunity to teach

Buzziness
IDEA

**Don't blend in
when you can
stand out!**

younger generations **business acumen**. That means it
was designed to teach kids how to think on their feet, deal
with business situations like handling money, and take
risks when selling a new product. So I went there with
eyes-wide-open enthusiasm. I was ready to learn it all.

On the day of the Acton Children's Business Fair, my
mom came into my bedroom and said she had a surprise
for me. From behind her back, she revealed a yellow-and-
black bee costume, with bee arms, bee legs, leg warmers,
bee hands, bee feet, wings, a tutu, and, yes, antennae. My
mom also gave me my first pair of honey bee earrings made
by her mom, Grandma Barbara. Grandma Barbara always
was busy making me honey and lemon jewelry. My mom
was excited for me to wear my bee costume. I remember
it being itchy, and it definitely wasn't my style, but as long
as it attracted customers, I guessed it was all right. "Why
blend in when you can stand out?" she said with a joyful
laugh. I realized that was a key lesson in business. I will
repeat it, because it's that important: *Why blend in when*

you can stand out? It's simple advice but often forgotten, especially as businesses begin to grow and are less willing to take risks.

When the very first Acton Children's Business Fair began, there were only seven kids and about twenty-five attendees. Two years later, when I arrived in my dad's car packed full of lemonade supplies, it had doubled, and today there are even more booths. It had grown quickly. Now, Acton business fairs are held all over the world, with hundreds of kids participating. It's a great way to get your feet wet when starting your own business.

The fair was located at what looked like a big house in a big yard with row after row of little white tents. When we pulled up to unload my supplies, I was surprised at how many kids were participating with some really great ideas and products to sell. They were selling things like foam lightsabers, fancy cookies, unusual jewelry, and gummy sushi. I wanted to go around to the different sellers and buy some of their products. Just as I started to visit different tents, someone announced the fair was starting in twenty minutes. I had to get to work.

Each participant was given a simple white table to display and sell their products. I set up my lemonade dispenser in the middle of the table, cups on one side of the table and cash box on the other. I had twenty dollars in small bills and coins in my cash box reserved for change. My mom kept arranging and rearranging the items on the table. Had I forgotten anything? Would I have enough change for customers? It was hot out—would the heat make my lemonade taste funny? It was too late for it to matter now. My father said I looked nervous. He suggested I come up with some ice breakers for when I sold to customers. I had read a few jokes about bees when I was doing my bee research, so I tried a couple of them out on customers when they came to my booth.

"Why did the bee go to the dermatologist?"

"Why?" he asked.

"Because it had hives."

And this one got a good laugh:

"What did the sushi say to the bee?"

Answer: "Wasabi!"

I had planned on selling my lemonade for a dollar a cup that day, but after seeing the prices of the other products being sold at the fair, we decided just as we were starting the event to increase the price to two dollars a cup. This was a business lesson, and one worth knowing: When considering the price of your product, study the market and know what the market can bear.

My first customers were a few kids also participating in the fair. I sold three cups of lemonade to them, then they asked me about the bees. I told them my story. It was easy talking to kids. But then adults started to show up, asking more questions. I explained what I knew about the bees. One adult told me some facts I didn't know. "Did you know that honey bees are one of the only insects that make food for people to eat?" I wasn't aware of that, so I wrote it down. Then I responded, "And did you know that honey bees pollinate fifty to one hundred flowers during their collection of pollen?" I liked the exchange of information.

It might just seem like casual conversation, but it felt like more to me than that. I was not only talking to people about a problem I was interested in solving, but I was educating others, and they were educating me. It was the first time in my young life where I felt like both a teacher and a student—and I liked that feeling. And, in a way, I also felt like I was speaking for the bees that day. A teenager came over who didn't have two dollars for my lemonade but wanted to donate what he did have to the bees. He didn't have any information to provide me; he just liked the idea of saving a small, delicate insect with an enormous impact on our society.

My parents were telling me to work on my math skills, so I was busy counting change when two more people came over and gave money just for the bees. I was surprised by how willing my customers were to listen and share their own bee-sting stories. One woman took a big gulp of my lemonade and said it was the best she'd ever tasted, and then, with a smile, said, "And it tastes even better with a good cause attached."

"Ohh, it's good!" another person said, finishing his cup, a little surprised by the different ingredients.

"Because I make it with love." I smiled. My bee costume's antennae danced in the air as I spoke.

I ran out of lemonade within a couple hours, which was disappointing. I was just getting started.

"I wish I had made more lemonade," I told my parents as we packed up early.

"There are only so many lemons you can squeeze, Mikaila," my father said.

What also made it difficult was that part of my recipe called for warming up some of the ingredients ahead of time, then cooling them down, so we couldn't make it on-site. I would have to figure out how to make more available next time.

At the business fair you can win awards like Most Creative Product, Most Likely to Succeed, Best Presentation, Best Customer Service, and Best Business Potential. I didn't win an award that year. I'd try again the next year. Winning or not winning wasn't really the point of the fair, because I came away with something that would turn out to be much more valuable than an award. I got a taste of what it meant to run a business, and I liked it very much. I was also able to learn about how other kids were running their companies and what creative ideas they had thought of.

It was now September 2009. It had been six months since my first bee sting. I was about to turn five. That night after the business fair, I made my first contribution to the bees.

I put a twenty-dollar bill in an envelope and addressed it to the Texas Beekeepers Association. The second donation I made was thirty dollars to Heifer International for one beehive for a family in a developing nation. I wondered what one beehive could do for a family—turns out, a lot! Bees pollinate the plants and crops in the area, and one single bee colony can double the amount of fruit and vegetables that are grown. Families can harvest not just the honey but also beeswax. In addition to being good to eat, honey has antiseptic properties for treating burns and cuts. People can use honey for skin care because of its ability to retain moisture. Beeswax, it turns out, isn't just for making candles. I was surprised to learn that it is just as valuable as honey, if not more so. The chemical makeup of beeswax makes it very stable, insoluble in water, and an excellent fuel. And yes, it has a high melting point, so it's perfect for candles. For families in developing nations, having a hive that produces honey and beeswax that can be sold or traded is invaluable. I wasn't just giving to the bees; I was giving to other communities.

As I started to read more about the benefits of donating just one single beehive, I began to think what change I could make with just one lemonade stand. What impact would I have with more lemonade stands?

I told my family I wanted to make more lemonade. A lot more. And I wanted to be ready for big events, like the next Lemonade Day, when all of Austin knew kids were selling lemonade for causes. I could really save the bees that day!

CHAPTER THREE

Building and Growing

After the fair,
I was so excited that all I could
think about was saving the bees. For the
next several months, I looked for every opportunity I
could to get my lemonade into the hands of new customers. I took lemonade with me to church and school
events—I was now in kindergarten, so many days I would
bring a large thermos to school and offer samples to students in my classroom. Lucky for me, Austin is always hot.
I'm told Austin is one of the sunniest cities in America.
All those sunny days gave opportunities for people to get
outside and try some lemonade, and, yes, for bees to pollinate. So even in the wintertime in Austin, people would
be thirsty for lemonade.

One of the counselors at my school had a family-owned farm-to-table restaurant called the 24 Diner. One day I was explaining to her my mission to save the bees by selling lemonade and asked if I could sell some lemonade to her. She suggested something better: Why didn't I set up my lemonade stand outside their restaurant to get more exposure? Even a kindergartner knows that's a good business opportunity, so I said yes immediately.

I prepared even more batches than at the fair and got quite a few restaurant customers during popular weekend brunch hours! They would buy their lemonade at my stand and then bring it in with them when they had their meal. With more traffic to my stand, I learned new things about my customers—like how they enjoyed a healthy version of lemonade and how my mission made them feel good about buying my product. Later we joked it was my first business partnership, and the best part was, I didn't have to pay rent.

One evening in November, after selling lemonade outside the restaurant, I said to my parents, "I want to go big on Lemonade Day."

My parents looked at each other.

Lemonade Day was in May, six months away. I didn't know it at the time, but I was strategizing the growth of my business by working toward goals as part of that process. Even at age five, I knew I had to set little goals for myself along the way, and it's something for you to think about as

well: *Create challenges and milestones. It will help motivate you as you grow your business.*

"I mean big, big. I want to buy one of those huge lemonade stands, and I want to sell tons of lemonade to all of Austin for the bees."

Buzziness IDEA

Create challenges and milestones. It will help motivate you as you grow your business.

There's this story my parents tell about me when I was an infant. I guess I used to cry really hard whenever they put me in my car seat. I hated car rides. Every single time they even started to put me in a car, I would wail. One time, my dad's parents came to town for the weekend. They kept telling my mother and father that they could stop me from crying by bundling me tighter or playing soothing music. But nothing worked. I still cried. Eventually even my grandparents gave up. Then one day my mom figured it out. It wasn't that I didn't like riding in the car; it was that I didn't like to face backward in my car seat. I wanted to face forward. Once the car seat was turned around when I was the appropriate age, I stopped crying. I guess I liked feeling like I was moving forward all the time, not backward.

The same was true with my lemonade stand. I couldn't look back. I had already started a little lemonade stand; I had grown to selling in front of a restaurant. Now I wanted to move forward with my business.

I had been setting up lemonade stands a few times a month—mostly on the weekends, since I was focused on school during the week—and I was making regular trips to the bank to deposit earnings into my savings account. I enjoyed watching the money in my account grow when I sold lemonade and then shrink as I donated more beehives.

More enjoyable was keeping track of the number of hives I donated by drawing a hive on my calendar every time I gave. However, while I was squeezing tons of lemons in those days, setting up stands, making some money, and donating to the bees, I wasn't really keeping close track of my budget at that point, or my **revenue**. Revenue is the amount of money that is earned by a company or organization. One day I noticed my hands were extra sore from handling the lemons all day. I had heard that if you roll a lemon on a hard surface, it softens the lemon and makes it easier to squeeze. So I rolled and squeezed, rolled and squeezed, and rolled and squeezed some more. I soon realized that I had outgrown the handheld lemon juicer, craft table, and other materials that I had started with. I needed to at least upgrade my lemon juicer from handheld to electric.

I asked my dad if we could go to the store and buy a fancy electric squeezer.

That's when my parents told me that if I wanted to go shopping for new materials, like an electric squeezer, I would have to make a **budget** and be sure not to overspend.

A budget is an estimate of costs and income set for a period of time.

"Is an electric juicer in your budget? *And* a lemonade stand?" my dad asked.

I shrugged. After all, I was only five years old then and had no idea really what a budget was. I had heard the word before because my dad was always talking about budgets. He's a finance guy, which means he works with numbers and money a lot, so he was always saying something was in our budget or out of our budget. I never understood that. To a little kid, it seemed like all you needed to do was put a plastic card in a machine and get whatever money you wanted.

"Are budgets really important? What if I don't do a budget?" I asked.

"If you don't do a budget, then you could spend all your money on a lemon squeezer and not have enough to upgrade other things you'll need in the future."

I didn't know the first thing about creating a budget, so my dad wrote down five steps on the dry-erase board in my bedroom and explained each step to me.

FIVE STEPS TO CREATING A BUDGET

STEP 1 **ESTIMATE YOUR INCOME.** This is where I estimated how much money I could make (**income**) by selling my lemonade in front of a restaurant and in my front yard for an hour or so.

2 **LIST YOUR EXPENSES. Expenses** are what you have to purchase. I wanted to upgrade my juicer and my lemonade stand, and I needed more ingredients, so by looking online and at the grocery store, we added up how much I'd have to spend.

3 **SUBTRACT YOUR EXPENSES FROM YOUR INCOME.** This is when math skills come in handy! Here I would subtract the total cost of all the things I'd have to buy from the money I'd make at the stand. This is how you find out whether or not you've made a profit (gained more than you've spent) or a loss (lost money).

4 **FIND WAYS TO REDUCE COST AND INCREASE SALES.** This is when I had to put my thinking cap on and brainstorm ways to attract more customers and spend less money. By doing this, you can increase your profit.

5 **SET GOALS.** Just like my mom had said at my first lemonade stand, it's important to set goals for yourself to keep you motivated! Some of my first goals were to be more outgoing when speaking to customers and think of ways to meet new customers and grow my business.

REVENUE – COST = PROFIT
increase this   or reduce this   to increase this

Profit, then, is what you have left after you've allocated money to the growth of your business.

So, first, we examined my business's budget items. We had a good-tasting, authentic recipe, a regular list of supplies, and had priced out all my ingredients. This was part of working within my budget, which meant I had first to list all the items required to make my lemonade—lemon squeezer, cups, water, lemons, flaxseed, honey, ice, etc. Then I needed to think about the materials I needed for promoting my product, such as a fancy colorful flyer and copies of that flyer. I had to understand how much everything would cost. Plus, I really, really wanted a professional lemonade stand, not just a folding table like at the Acton Children's Business Fair. So I went online to see what a lemonade stand would cost. They weren't cheap. The one I liked the most cost $145. It was pink and official-looking, and I loved it. With the $145 lemonade stand, $70 for ingredients, $15 for a new electric juicer, and $25 for marketing materials, my budget was $255.

Before I got too far ahead of myself, my dad said, "When you're thinking about a budget, you need to start backward."

As you know, backward and I don't go well together. I was confused. Start backward?

"You don't start with how much it will cost to buy a lemonade stand online and all the ingredients, supplies, and marketing materials," he said.

I was still confused.

"You start by asking yourself how much you want to sell your lemonade for," he said.

Money is a pretty difficult concept to most kids. I had sold it before for a dollar, so to keep it simple, I said, "A dollar?"

"Okay, let's take a dollar and start backward," he said.

I nodded. It didn't really make sense to me, but I played along.

"How many cups of lemonade do you want to sell?" he said.

"I guess sixty?" I don't know where I came up with that number, but I remembered my mom commenting that that was probably the most we could sell in an afternoon without getting tired.

"Okay," my father said, and started writing down the math. "At a dollar per cup, how much money will you make if you sell sixty cups?"

He helped me figure out we would make sixty dollars.

"But if you want to buy your lemonade stand and have money for supplies, marketing materials, and new equipment, which you determined will cost you two hundred fifty-five dollars, will sixty be enough?"

"No?" I said.

"You're correct," my dad said. "The answer is no. You

won't have enough money if you only sell your lemonade for a dollar."

I was getting it … kind of.

He tried again. "Do you want the number in the bank to go up or down?"

I said I wanted the number to go up.

"Yes. Then you want to earn at least a dollar *more* than you spend on supplies, equipment, and marketing. Remember, that's called profit." I like profit.

My father explained that if we sold my lemonade for a dollar, it would not leave me with a profit, but a loss.

"If you want all these budget items"—he started scribbling down numbers on a piece of paper—"you have to sell each cup of lemonade for four dollars and twenty-seven cents to make a profit after spending two hundred fifty-five dollars."

"Okay, let's do it!"

My father laughed. "Don't you think four dollars and twenty-seven cents is a little costly for a small cup of lemonade?"

He explained that I could only sell my lemonade for so much money before it became too expensive for people to want to buy, and $4.27 would certainly turn customers away. So I needed to find a way to make a profit *and* lower my costs.

"What if I sold my lemonade for two dollars a cup?" I said.

Starting backward, if I sold sixty cups of lemonade for $2 and made sales of $120, I still wouldn't have enough.

Steps to Creating a Budget

REVENUE   ORIGINAL PLAN

Sales $120

BUDGET ITEM	PLAN
Ingredients	$70
Equipment (Juicer) . .	$15
Property (Stand)	$145
Marketing	$25
TOTAL	$255
Profit/Loss	-$135

My dad said, "Based on your budget, you need to figure out a way to lower your costs."

"How do I do that?"

We went back to my idea of the lemonade stand I wanted to buy online. At $145, it took up a lot of my budget. So I couldn't buy it—at least not at this stage in my business. I quickly learned the concept of **build versus buy**. This is an expression often used to describe the decision to create something in-house or purchase it from an outside source. My dad was pretty handy. He had built the deck on our house, made me a wooden rocking horse, and built my brother an awesome fire truck bed. I asked if he could build a lemonade stand for me within my budget. He said it was possible, so we headed to Home Depot and got wood and paint for only $20—quite a difference from the $145 it would cost me for the premade one online. All in one day, I helped him design a simple stand and he built it. My dad did the lettering. On the top of the stand he painted FRESH LEMONADE, with some colorful swirls and a big lemon. It was beautiful!

It was so much fun working on a project with my dad. Plus, I saved a ton of money, and I actually liked the stand

we designed better than the premade ones online. I learned a valuable lesson: If you can build it yourself, go for it. It's more meaningful in the end.

Next, the honey. Honey was the most expensive ingredient in my lemonade. Maybe I could save there. I didn't want to use regular store-bought honey, though, because in doing research, I'd read that by buying local honey, you help the bees, and also the environment, of your own city because your money stays local and you're investing in a local farm. I knew that I wanted to buy locally, but local honey was very expensive. I would have to figure out how to get that cost down. I couldn't afford the expensive honey sold at farms and co-op markets, so I went to a local beekeeper named Konrad at Round Rock Honey farm near my home and asked if I could use his honey for my lemonade. He agreed and suggested that I share that our product was sweetened with Round Rock Honey. That's called **bartering**. Bartering is when you exchange something you want for something you can provide, instead of using money. This might be products, like honey, or a service, like mowing the lawn, for other goods or services. In this case, I got Konrad's honey in exchange for promoting his brand.

Next, the marketing materials. Photocopying full-color flyers was expensive. So instead, I bought a few poster boards and drew some handmade signs with markers.

With those few adjustments, I ended up getting my overall budget down from $255 to $75. Not bad, I thought. If I charged $2 for a cup of lemonade, I would only need to sell thirty-eight cups to turn a profit. Here's the math: 38 cups × 2 = $76. I'd make only $1 profit, but I knew I could easily sell more than thirty-eight cups at one of my lemonade stands. My goal was sixty. If I made a large profit, I would use some of my earnings to buy a fancy electric juicer for $15. Squeezing would go twice as fast, and I would be able to produce even more lemonade.

All of that effort of getting ready took me a few months in between school, after-school activities, holidays, dance recitals, and all the usual things that kids do—like play with friends! Finally, with a fun new handmade lemonade stand, colorful posters, and a budget, I was ready for Lemonade Day in May, just a month away!

"Not yet," my mother said.

What now? I thought.

"You need an elevator pitch."

What on earth do elevators have to do with selling lemonade?

An **elevator pitch** is something everyone needs when

selling something—whether it's lemonade or glitter slime. The name comes from the idea that you have only thirty seconds with someone in an elevator to get them interested in your product before they reach their floor. I needed to think about who my lemonade was for (everyone!), what it did (satisfy thirst), why it was needed (healthy alternative to soft drinks and would save the bees), and how I made it (by hand, with love).

My pitch: Through my lemonade, I hope to inspire people in our community to drink and eat healthier and to take action to help secure our food supply by saving one of our most important pollinators—the bees!

Finally, I needed more practice selling my lemonade. So I posted some of my signs all over the neighborhood to get people to my lemonade stand.

For a few weekends, I set up my lemonade stand in front of my house, and told people how I made the lemonade and why it was important to buy my lemonade. I also promoted the beekeeper's honey and emphasized the importance of saving the bees. Then I told them to come back on Lemonade Day to offer the bees more support!

I got comfortable talking to strangers—I know parents tell their kids not to talk to strangers, but my parents were right there with me scooping the ice, so it felt safe. It was fun meeting new people and seeing them smile when they tried my product. And I really liked teaching them about the bees, pollination, the importance of bees in our food chain, and the ingredients I used to make my lemonade.

And I especially liked it when they bought a cup and I got to take the money.

Buzziness IDEA

Know your product and be able to get someone interested in it quickly. Don't be afraid to tell them what makes it unique and why they might need it.

Since my first lemonade stand in my front yard almost a year earlier, I'd become really good at selling lemonade, so that when Lemonade Day rolled around, I was more than ready to raise money for the bees. And at five and a half years old, a little over a year after being stung by two bees, I had not only learned a lot about the bees, but I had a unique product, a business name, a savings account, a budget, an official-looking lemonade stand, marketing materials, an elevator pitch, tons of information about bees, and enough lemonade for the whole day.

I had participated in my first official Lemonade Day, and I ended up selling all sixty cups of lemonade by the afternoon for a total of $120. I also earned enough money to finally buy my doll.

It was the start of something new!

CHAPTER FOUR

Bees Take Flight

After that first Lemonade Day in May 2010, I continued to look for more events to sell my lemonade. I was still only five and a half, and I didn't really know what it meant to grow a company, but what I did know was that mine wasn't really growing that much.

"Don't be discouraged. It takes a while to grow," my mom would say to me on days when not many people would stop by my stand.

It's true. If there's one thing I've learned about building a business, it's that it takes time, patience, and a lot of love for what you're doing. You'll experience that, too. Sometimes there will be rapid growth, sometimes very little growth. It's important to understand that it will fluctuate.

There were days when I wouldn't sell many cups of lemonade and I would get frustrated. Other days I would sell lemonade, but customers would try my product and would criticize it: "It's too sour." I was always questioning and wanting to improve my product. Maybe I needed to make it sweeter? Then someone would come along and say, "It's too sweet." It was confusing.

A business lesson I learned in my early days of making and selling lemonade: You can't possibly please everyone, so don't try. What you can do, and what I learned to do, was to stay true to my mission and focus on helping to save the bees. The way you do that is to *create a product that appeals to the most people.* This is important to remember. Sometimes we can get wrapped up in ideas that sound great at the time but might not interest many buyers. My original flower Play-Doh balls that I made when I was four years old are a great example of that. Who wants a flower Play-Doh ball? And what do you do with a flower Play-Doh ball? Nothing. You need to create a product that is sellable and will allow you to raise more money toward your cause. Whether people like your product or not, you're still educating them about what is most important to you.

"It takes steadiness to build a business from the ground up," my dad would say. Then he would add with a smile, "Steadiness and grace."

I was in one of those steady-growth phases in my lemonade stand business when I participated in a lemonade contest at the Austin Children's Museum at six years old.

Bu**zz**iness
IDEA

Create a product that appeals to the most people. You can't please everyone, so don't try. Stay true to your mission and focus on helping your mission.

There were only about fifteen or so other contestants, so it wasn't a very big event, but I ended up winning the top award for Most Creative Lemonade, which was very exciting for me, because it was the first time I'd won an award for my lemonade, and I received a big gold trophy.

But the best part of all was that I got interviewed on a local television news station for winning. I remember standing there in my bee costume and speaking to the news reporter with excitement and nervousness. He asked me my age and questions about my lemonade. I stood there in front of the camera in my little bee suit and looked him right in the

eye, answering all his questions about donating a portion of my earnings toward saving the bees and how I created a unique product that was healthy and delicious. I was too afraid to look into the camera.

Afterward my family and I went out for ice cream, but all I remember thinking was that I wanted to get home to watch myself on television. It was a strange and exciting sensation to see myself on TV. I wondered how many people were watching me, too, and if they'd come to my lemonade stand to buy my drink for the bees.

For several months after that, I continued to set up my lemonade stand at events or in my front yard on weekends, and I did lots of free workshops on how to save the bees and educated more people. I even did another Acton Children's Business Fair—on a very windy day (and again didn't win any awards)—and another Lemonade Day, where I made a good amount of money and raised awareness about the bees. I was happy selling lemonade and donating to the charities, but I wondered if there could be more than just lemonade stands.

Then, when I was seven years old, during an Austin Lemonade Day—the third one I had participated in at this point—Michael Freid, the co-owner of East Side Pies, a really delicious pizza place in Austin, came over and tried my lemonade.

He said, "Your lemonade is really good. Have you ever thought of putting it in a bottle?"

When he said that, instantly a light bulb went off in my head. I hadn't considered bottling my lemonade before that, but maybe this was a way to achieve my goal of growing my business.

"If your lemonade was in a bottle, I'd sell it in my restaurant."

My eyes got wide with excitement. Someone was offering me a way to raise much more money for the bees!

I thanked him for the offer, a little stunned.

After he left my stand, I looked at my dad and said, "I want to sell lemonade in stores year-round and not just at events a few times a year. Do you know how much money I could raise for the bees?"

My dad said thoughtfully, "It is a good idea. Let's figure it out." When he said those words, my whole mood changed. I was overjoyed!

For the next week, I was floating from the thought of bottling my lemonade. Soon after the conversation with the owner of East Side Pies, my dad and I were driving home from school, and I said to him casually, "So when are we going to figure out how to bottle my lemonade?" I knew even as a seven-year-old that I couldn't push my parents too hard on something this big.

"Oh, are you still thinking about that?" my dad said with a sideways glance and a smile.

"Yes! Let's do it."

"Come on," he said, "let's go see how other beverages are doing it."

A few moments later, my dad was turning into the parking lot of a neighborhood grocery store.

At the store, my dad asked where the bottled beverages were. There was a large selection of bottled cold drinks. Noticing our curiosity, the manager came over and offered to answer all of our questions. We asked her if they had any lemonades. I told the manager that I sold lemonade at my stand and wanted to sell it in bottles. The store manager took us very seriously and spent quite a bit of time looking at different products in the cold box, explaining what she liked about each one. She gave us recommendations and things to think about if we were going to go into bottling—packaging type, label design, ingredients. There were a few recommendations that she felt very strongly about—one was that we should use glass bottles, and another was that the ingredients needed to be simple and natural. She also suggested a local commercial kitchen that we should contact, called SASS.

My family and I didn't know the first thing about bottling beverages. So we went home and started doing lots of online research.

It seemed pretty straightforward at first, but there were a lot more things involved than just getting juice into a bottle, sticking a label on, and capping it.

"You know, Mikaila," my mom said to me as we were scrolling through different bottling options on the internet, "bottling means it will no longer be just a lemonade stand when you have time in the summer and on weekends."

But I kept pushing the number of bottles we'd need.

"Maybe we should buy five hundred bottles!" I said. "I mean because it's cheaper to buy in bulk." I was catching on.

"If you're really serious about investing this kind of time—" my dad said.

"I am!" I said firmly.

"If you're really serious about investing this kind of time *and* money *and* long-term commitment," he continued, looking me in the eye, "then we need to come up with a business plan."

I had no idea what that was, but I said, "You're on!"

Seven-year-olds don't normally deal with business plans in daily life, but my parents were both businesspeople, and business plans were part of their regular lives. They knew that every good company needed a business plan from the very beginning.

Your company needs a **business plan**, too, no matter how small. Here is why: The purpose of a business plan is to create a roadmap for yourself *before* you grow, because you'll find that when growing a business, you'll often get distracted by new things that come up. A business plan will force you to ask yourself important questions about your business, like who you are and what you want to do with your company. It will give you a chance to think about your goals, your values, your mission, and most importantly, it will help keep you on track.

Having a plan that's written down also forces a level of discipline that is essential as your business becomes more complicated. If your business is growing quickly, you can refer to your business plan and remind yourself of where you want to direct your energy. It's also a way to crystallize thoughts and ideas and understand what you're doing not only *before* you grow, but *while* you're growing.

My parents and I started with a simple business plan. Here are some things you should consider when creating your own business plan:

Buzziness
IDEA

A business plan is to create a roadmap for yourself before you grow. It will force you to ask yourself important questions; will give you a chance to think about your goals, your values, and your mission; and will help keep you on track.

- What is your company?
- What is the main thing you want your company to do (your mission)?
- What is the main thing you want your company to be known for (your vision)?
- What little things can you do to help you achieve your mission (your goals and objectives)?
- How are you going to achieve your vision (your strategic plan and focus)?
- What type of business field are you in (your industry)?
- How much will you sell and earn (your projections)?

This all seemed very overwhelming and confusing at the time, so my father walked me through a few steps in simple terms. In general, you need to know the identity of your business. How it got started and what makes it special. *Who was I as a business?* I was a girl who started a lemonade stand using a recipe inspired by my great-grandmother with the intention of helping endangered bees.

Your mission statement really identifies what the purpose of your business is and how you are going to measure your success. Your **mission** is your reason for being and forces you to ask yourself what the foundation of your company is. *My mission:* To raise money to help save the honey bees while encouraging people to drink lemonade.

Your **vision** statement should be about the big picture. It should be emotional and enthusiastic and original. What makes your company feel huge and awesome? *My vision:* To improve the world we live in by providing natural products that inspire environmental, social, and personal awareness.

Your **goal** is pretty straightforward and will change as your business grows. For example, do you want your product to be in one hundred stores by the end of the year? Do you want to get your costs down? *My goal:* Educate others about the importance of bees in our ecosystem while selling lemonade that makes people happy and healthy.

There were still things I needed to figure out to complete my business plan, but my parents and I agreed it was a good start. We would take some time to think about our long-term strategic plan, learn more about the industry, and consider our projections once we had some experience with East Side Pies. All this would come in time. There were other things to do.

Before I could even sell my bottles of lemonade in a pizza parlor, we had to be registered with the state as an official business. So we registered my company as "Mikaila's BeeSweet Lemonade," which officially made my business its own business entity.

"I just started a company!" I said to my little brother when I completed the paperwork.

"I want to help," he said. He was four at the time, and I was seven. We decided he would help me market my business.

"What does that mean?"

"I think it means you make posters."

"Okay!"

Now we needed to figure out how to get my lemonade into bottles.

Up until that point, I was producing lemonade in our kitchen and selling from my stand at different events. But as I grew, I became aware of something I hadn't expected. There were a lot of rules and regulations associated with selling a beverage product in retail stores and restaurants. For example, you have to list ingredients and provide a nutritional panel.

"How on earth do we calculate a nutritional panel?" my mom wondered.

We got back to work doing research. We found a free nutrition label generator online and downloaded the app. It started to calculate the ingredients immediately. Things like how many calories are in two cups of lemon juice and three tablespoons of honey. How many units and grams of sugar, what percentage of daily nutrition, protein, fiber. It calculated everything. It would then generate a basic nutritional panel or a high-end complex panel. We went with the basic nutritional panel. Then we created our own labels using clip art that said BEESWEET LEMONADE with a smiling bee flying through the air. We pasted the nutritional information on the back. I liked it, but it didn't look very professional. So we decided to ask what other people thought. I had a friend in school, Lily, whose mom was a graphic designer. Ms. Lori said she had some ideas and agreed to help us with designing a more professional-looking label. I wasn't really sure what I wanted the design to look like, so I just told her to make it look "lemonade-y."

When the design came back, it was so cool! She had done an illustration of my face and put BEESWEET LEMONADE in really pretty fonts and colors. It was a great business lesson. If it doesn't feel right or look right, keep going until you're thrilled with the results. I was very proud.

At first I felt a little awkward having my face on the label, and my parents felt a little protective of my identity— since I was still just a kid—but after some consideration, my

mom said something interesting: "Why not? Let them see who is speaking for the bees!" I did like the illustration of me because it made me look older, and I quickly got used to seeing my face on my bottles of lemonade. I was very proud to have it as a label.

Next, we needed to find the right packaging. Based on the suggestion from the manager at the grocery store near our house, we knew that we wanted glass bottles. I had been learning in school at the time about all the bits of plastic that were in the ocean and harming wildlife, so I wanted to go with a bottling option that was more environmentally friendly. We found a number of companies that sold bottles in different sizes and designs, but they required that you buy really large quantities. Some even required that you buy a full truckload—this would be the large eighteen-wheel trucks. We didn't want to make a huge investment in bottles at first, since we weren't really sure what we were doing. We didn't know how to solve this problem, so we began to call around to see if we could find a local source that could help.

We also had to tackle our biggest challenge—government regulations. The law said that we needed to create our product in a commercial kitchen that had been permitted for commercial use by the City of Austin. Which meant we couldn't make the lemonade out of our house if it was going to be sold at stores or in restaurants.

I think my whole family was relieved to hear we had to move our production line out of our house. Producing lemonade in large batches had overtaken our small kitchen. There was constant clutter from the ingredients, measuring cups, pitchers, and honey jars. And no matter how clean we kept our workspace, there still seemed to be sticky lemonade everywhere.

So we went searching for a commercial kitchen—also known as a **copacker**. You provide a copacker with your recipe and the ingredients and the packaging materials, and they will go from recipe to finished product. Surprisingly, a couple miles from our home was the small commercial kitchen, SASS, that the grocery store manager had recommended. We had driven by the building a million times, and it had never crossed my mind what was actually going on inside. Compared to making lemonade in our home kitchen, this place was huge!

The only problem was, we still weren't really large enough to need a full-time commercial kitchen, but if we were going to bottle and sell them in a restaurant, we needed to find someone who would take us. Through a series of discussions, the owners of SASS agreed to do a small run for us. They happened to be producing a salad dressing at the time and asked if we wanted to use that type of bottle as well. The larger the orders you place, the less expensive the bottles are, so it was a win for the salad dressing maker and for us. This solved two of our problems—we'd found a source for small glass orders and a copacker that met all of the legal requirements. These little details were key to a quick rollout. We also kept costs low by using their existing packaging materials and delivering the product ourselves.

We made our first official production run out of a commercial kitchen in February 2013. At eight years old, I got to see an entire assembly line of people making my recipe, and this was such a big deal to me. It was also a huge relief to hand this responsibility over to someone else because then I could focus more on telling my story and saving the bees and not have to worry about mixing large batches of lemonade.

Once we had a good product bottled, labeled, and chilled, I made my parents drive me to East Side Pies. It had been about nine months since I first met Michael Freid on Lemonade Day, but he remembered who I was the second I walked into the restaurant.

"I bottled my lemonade," I told him proudly. "And I'm taking orders!"

I gave him a sample bottle, and after taking a pretty long sip, he ordered thirty bottles of lemonade.

Mikaila's BeeSweet Lemonade was now in the bottling business.

Visiting with my new customers

CHAPTER FIVE

Going to Market

I had officially taken BeeSweet Lemonade to the next level: the market! Which meant I would be setting aside my lemonade stand for a while. It also meant I would need to think about how much lemonade I wanted to make and how much I wanted to grow my business. These were big questions for a little kid. While I was thinking about that, I also had to focus on other things in my life, like completing my leaf science experiment for school, studying my vocabulary words, and practicing for an upcoming dance recital.

I quickly discovered that there's a huge difference between mixing a few pitchers for a lemonade stand and producing a beverage in larger quantities. When bottling lemonade, you have to be much more detailed with your measurements—much more than I had expected.

The commercial kitchen would still mix, bottle, and label my lemonade, but I had to provide them with the ingredients and figure out exact measurements for bulk orders—which meant we had to make a completely new budget that included buying scales for weighing ingredients. And there was a lot of taste testing to make sure the lemonade was just right, and then we again had to judge batches based on color, smell, and consistency—which was actually one of my favorite parts. We also found that the taste of honey changes depending on the flowers that the bees pollinate, the amount of rain, and the time of year it was produced.

We noticed other things, too. My mom would say, "The color of this batch doesn't look right." I realized that the math I was learning in school, like multiplication, came in quite handy. If I wanted to double or triple the amount of lemonade I produced, I would need to do the same with each ingredient.

After taste testing, and tweaking my recipe, I would add new ingredients to my supply list. Once, as I was going through my new list of supplies, my father interrupted, "Do you have enough money to pay for these new supplies?" We went through the math of my new budget together. I didn't have enough money. Initially, I thought that in order to get the rest of the money, I needed to sell out of my stand again, but my dad gave me another option.

"What if you ask for a loan?" A **loan** is a sum of money borrowed with the expectation that it will be paid back.

"Usually someone might go to the bank and ask for a loan, but since it's not too much money you're asking for, I'll give you a loan," my dad said. I would need to pay him back, but he agreed not to charge **interest**. Interest is the money you would pay in addition to the amount that a bank or person lends you. Most all banks will charge you interest calculated at a particular rate, but my dad figured he could let this one slide.

I was only fifty dollars short from my estimated expenses, so I asked for a fifty-dollar loan from my parents. They were helping me learn that you need to make more money than you spend. That's what a profit is. And I still wanted extra money left over to give to bee organizations.

Even with a loan, we had to rethink how we purchased some of our ingredients. Lemons, for example. We would need a lot more of them. But they can be expensive if you're buying them individually at the grocery store; now we needed them in bulk.

The thing I learned about lemons, and fruit and vegetables in general, is that they might always be available in supermarkets, but if something like extreme weather hurts a crop during the growing season, prices skyrocket. For example, in 2018, there was a heat wave and a shortage of water in Southern California, one of the major lemon-growing regions in the United States. Prices for fresh lemons rose by a lot that year. Normally, a carton of lemons costs about thirty-six dollars. But after the heat wave, it cost closer to fifty-two dollars.

I couldn't afford to pay the higher prices for ingredients at the grocery store, so I learned the power of **negotiation**. When you negotiate with someone, you're working together to come to an agreement. Instead of buying a few lemons at the grocery store, I went to a **wholesaler**—a dealer who sells goods to stores or to businesses that make products sold in stores instead of directly to the public—and negotiated a price by buying in bulk. We were able to buy a whole case of lemons for a lower price. We were going to be using a lot of lemons, so this was a big win.

My first order to East Side Pies fed my ambition for selling my lemonade everywhere, all year. My parents expressed some concern about being able to balance school and the business, but they could see the excitement in my eyes.

"Okay," my dad said. "We'll figure it out." Within a couple weeks, East Side Pies was asking for more than I had produced in our commercial kitchen. We were selling more and more cases every week, and we had to increase the order size runs, which seemed large at the time. We quickly taught ourselves how to invoice East Side Pies using an online form—there are many free templates online! They would pay us by check up front... I liked that the most.

Some of the biggest questions when starting a business

are: How do I grow? How do I spread the word? And how do I manage that growth? The first three things you need to think about when growing your brand are:

1. Maintain customer loyalty—keep the customers you have happy.
2. Identify new opportunities.
3. Get your product into new customers' hands.

I kept those three thoughts in my mind as I bottled my lemonade. Managing my growth, I figured, would come with experience.

After a couple months exclusively fulfilling orders for East Side, I got an email from a store named Quickie Pickie. They explained they were located near East Side Pies and had tried my lemonade. They loved my product and asked if they could sell it as well. A new customer!

But excitement quickly turned to nervousness. Producing the lemonade was only part of the business. I knew that as I grew, I needed to get out there and meet people. I remembered the advice my mom gave me when I first started my lemonade stand—to get my product into as many people's hands as possible. So I used every opportunity I could to engage with possible new customers.

On one occasion, my mom and I went into TOM's Roasting Co. in Austin. They have the best peppermint hot chocolate with cardamom whipped cream, and I was craving one. When I ordered my drink, I overheard one woman say she was the manager of the store. I had an idea. After I got my hot chocolate, I asked to speak to the manager. When she came over, I told her about my lemonade. She was eager to try it.

"I happen to have a sample in my cooler in the car." I carried samples of my product everywhere. I brought her a bottle. She told me it tasted delicious and ordered two cases— twenty-four bottles.

"It's that easy?" I asked my mom in the car a few minutes later.

"Not always," she said with a laugh. I wanted to get my lemonade in more stores, so over the course of the next several weeks and months, after school and on weekends, I would visit coffee shops and cafés and introduce my product to store managers. My mom was right—it wasn't easy.

Buzziness
IDEA

Three things to think about when growing your brand:

1
KEEP YOUR CUSTOMERS HAPPY

2
IDENTIFY NEW OPPORTUNITIES

3
GET YOUR PRODUCT INTO NEW CUSTOMERS' HANDS

Some places turned me down outright. They'd say that my company was too small or they didn't have enough space on their shelves. Some didn't even think my product would sell. And some were interested but never called me back.

Then a reporter from our local newspaper walked into one of the stores that carried my lemonade, bought a bottle, and called to interview me and my family for a story about my mission to save the bees. I remember jumping up and down while my mom and the reporter were conversing about the potential story. They were very interested in my mission to save the bees.

After the article ran, a few stores contacted us to order my lemonade. Then the City of Austin called to sell my lemonade at their visitor center. One day I got a call from the W Austin hotel. They said they'd love to carry my product because we shared a mission to save the bees.

The hotel even had glassed-in beehives at their rooftop restaurant and thought it would be cool to market a lemonade made with local honey (even if it wasn't the honey being made on the roof). It was such a unique hotel, and I finally realized why my mom had told me to always create a special product or service. People love unusual experiences in life.

As sales increased, I needed to keep track of them. I made sure that I noted every expense and every check that I deposited from selling my lemonade. This way I could track my money and make sure I was making a profit, while also setting aside money toward the bees.

We started visiting grocery stores, too. The managers would talk to me about types of bottles, ingredients, and flavors, and one store even put us in contact with other local beverage companies. I had no idea so many other people were bottling beverages. That was something I wasn't expecting, but a lesson you should know before diving in. *Know your competition.*

In almost every industry or product, you will have to compete against other companies for customers. That is why it is crucial that you make your product unique and offer

Buzziness
IDEA

Before creating your business: Know your competition.

something new. It can be a new twist on an old or current product, but it has to be seen as an upgrade, and it has to stand out.

There are hundreds of bottled lemonade companies. But my ingredients, my story, and my mission to save the bees make mine special. To research your competition, you can:

- Visit stores and see if there are similar products.
- Conduct polls online or survey family, friends, and neighbors to ask if anybody has heard of products or services similar to yours.
- Research online for similar products and get their sales history.

Gathering information about your competitors is really important because you need to establish a need or want for your product to ensure ahead of time that you will have customers.

Even after our initial run with our commercial kitchen, owners of stores and restaurants kept coming back with more and more orders. With sales at the pizza parlor, coffee shops, Austin's visitor center, and the W Austin doing well, word started to get out that my product was helping to raise money to save the bees. The commercial kitchen started doing larger runs for us more regularly, and we realized without knowing it in the moment that we were growing—and quickly! At that point,

Testing lemonade!

we only had a simple website that my mom had designed, and my contact information was on the back of our bottle. Originally, the only way buyers could get in touch with me was to call my parents. During dinner one night, my mom said, "We need to create a better website."

She explained that having a stronger online presence wasn't just about providing information to customers, it offered a larger audience accessibility to our story, made us look more professional, and most important to me, it gave me a way to share my mission to save the bees.

With a lot of help from Ms. Lori, my friend Lily's mom, we started the design process by flagging our favorite websites: what layouts we found most pleasing, fonts we liked, colors we loved, how much content and how many images we wanted per page. Since a company's homepage acts as a first impression to buyers, what did we want that to look like—professional yet playful and inviting. How many tabs did we want to have in the pulldown menu? Did we want to link our website to other websites? And then there was content to write. Once you launch a website, it has to remain fresh. Someone would need to write content on a regular basis. Shortly after we launched our website, my mom started my social media pages. Managing the website and social media became another job in our already-packed schedules. But our website became a nice base that we would enjoy developing and adding to over time. We also heard from a lot of other people who wanted to save the bees.

CHAPTER SIX

Growing with the Bees

I was in third grade when we would go to the commercial kitchen on a regular basis after school to check in on production. My little brother, Jacob, who was just five years old at the time, would tag along. He was full of energy and couldn't keep his hands off the equipment. I noticed Jacob was getting into everything.

"Was I like that at Jacob's age?" I asked my mom.

She laughed. "That's the way kids learn, by getting into everything. Muddy hands and face mean you're seeing how things work," she said. We learn through our five senses, experiencing the world through sight, touch, taste, smell, and sound. I realized something very critical was missing

Buzziness IDEA

Understand why you are creating your product and have a deep appreciation for it.

with my business. I had given $225 and twenty volunteer hours to the bees, and I was seeing how my lemonade was made, but I had never actually seen how bees lived, how their hives worked, and how honey was made other than in videos. The more I thought about it, the more I wanted to learn even more about the bees. I needed to visit their hives, and not just visit, but study up close and learn. To be able to understand every component, every working piece of your business, is critical for the success of your mission.

We went back to Konrad, the local beekeeper at Round Rock Honey farm, who provided the honey for our lemonade, and I signed up for a beekeeping course. The first thing people see when they get to Round Rock is all the wildflowers. Fields of flowers as far as the eye can see. And bees darting everywhere! I was a little nervous at first—there really were a lot of bees, and though I'd grown to love them, I still hadn't quite gotten over my fear of being stung. After a quick tutorial, Konrad suited me up.

Because I was so young, and the only child they'd ever had who took a beekeeping course, none of the bee suits fit me. The smallest suit they put on me was droopy and therefore didn't offer much protection against the bees, so he doubled up the suits. They rolled up my sleeves to make it tighter and put on gloves that went all the way up to my

elbows. And I wore boots. I felt pretty well protected, but the two suits were very heavy, and it was very hot.

Konrad led me to an active hive. He explained that each bee colony had anywhere from twenty thousand to sixty thousand honey bees and only one queen. Worker bees are female—they do all the work. Male bees are drones, and their job is to mate. Konrad handed me the smoker, which smokes away the bees and prevents them from attacking us. The smoke interrupts their sense of smell and masks the alarm released by guard bees during a beekeeper's inspection. The smoke creates an opportunity for the beekeeper to open the hive and work while the colony's defensive response is down.

"Now," he said through a cloud of smoke, "let's collect some honey." We lifted the frames, and he pointed out the queen bee, who was dancing in a circle. She was much larger than the worker bees. The queen is the largest bee in the colony, usually measuring around twenty millimeters long (about three-quarters of an inch). Funny thing is, compared to the size of her body, her wings are much shorter than the other bees'. Probably because she's too busy laying eggs to do any flying. Queen bees lay an average of two thousand eggs a day and don't leave the hive.

All of these facts led to more questions in my mind, like what happens when the queen bee dies? And how many flowers does it take to make honey? Being part of the process and guided by a professional beekeeper answered a lot of my questions.

Checking on the bees in their hives

A bee smoker helps calm the bees before opening the hive

To make one pound of honey, honey bees will collect the pollen of two million flowers. When the queen bee dies, the hive could die. But if it's noticed in time, you can help save the hive by introducing a new queen from outside the hive. Bees have to keep the inside of the hive at 95°F, and there needs to be enough of them in the hive to keep it warm. If it is not warm enough, the bees will not make eggs and egg larvae. All bees are fed some royal jelly the first few days after they hatch, but the queen is the only one that feeds on royal jelly her whole life. This is what makes a queen bee as opposed to worker bees. Royal jelly is a lot like honey but more cloudy. It's produced by honey bees to feed the queen bee, which is where it gets the name.

Konrad showed me where the honey is formed and where the pollen is stored in a hive. He would point out something new, then hop over to a different active hive. He popped over to many hives throughout the day.

I couldn't help but think his darting around was influenced by the bees he so clearly loved. There were lots of them in multiple glass and steel structures, so it was easy to see how the term "busy bee" came about. And there was so much to do.

"Ants love honey," Konrad said as he worked. "They want the honey and mess up the wax. That's why beehives never touch the ground." For hives that were close to the ground, beekeepers would sprinkle a ring of cinnamon around the hives. "Ants love honey, but they hate cinnamon," Konrad explained.

I had way more appreciation for the hard work of bee-keepers after my course at Round Rock Honey.

I also had a deeper appreciation for the importance of native wildflowers, which helped to create so many different varieties and flavors of honey. I learned that the taste of honey changes season to season, depending on what the bees are pollinating. That was very important information to understand when I was creating my product. Clover, for instance, tastes different than lavender. I decided when I got home, I was going to start my own apiary. Apiaries are places where a collection of beehives are kept.

"No," my parents both said jointly. "That's way too much work." Instead we decided to plant bee-friendly flowers all over our yard: purple coneflowers, verbena, sweet acacia, and salvia. The flowers also brought more butterflies.

Around that same time in school, we were learning about monarch butterflies and their migration south. Monarch butterflies cannot live in cold climates and wouldn't survive the cold winters of most of the United States, so they migrate south and west each autumn to the warmer climates of Mexico and Southern California. They like to hibernate in the same trees every year, which makes for some pretty impressive scenes.

Like the bees, monarch butterflies are in decline due to people cutting down large portions of forest areas. I learned that many of the beautiful insects that are so helpful in pollinating the food and flowers that we love are in decline and need our help.

I began to think about ecosystems and animals differently, and I shared this with my classmates and teachers. I also began to wonder about the importance of other animals in our ecosystems. Were their populations diminishing like the bees'? Why do butterflies matter? Like bees, they are one of our great pollinators. But what about other animals, like ducks? And songbirds. What about turtles and dogs? Why do they matter? I was starting to understand. We are all connected, we all matter. Thoughts surrounding the mission of my lemonade business shifted as well. I was seeing a bigger picture. Why does one beehive donation matter? Because it's one more colony of bees pollinating flowers, and one more beehive making honey and producing wax. Sometimes one small change opens the possibility for more change.

I also came to understand that it becomes a lot more enjoyable to build a business when you not only have hands-on experience and know-how, but passion. Every business leader needs to get their hands dirty, or in my case, sticky. Here is why: When you're really dedicated to something, it shows. You can't fake passion. The one big lesson I've learned, however: You have to believe in your product and you must be committed to your mission. Your product might change and evolve and improve over time or in order

Buzziness **IDEA**

It's a lot more enjoyable to build a business when you have hands-on experience, know-how, and passion.

to fit the needs of today's consumers—but you need to be dedicated.

A few weeks after my beekeeping course, I went back to visit Konrad and Round Rock Honey, and I was surprised to see the farm looked very different. Bad flooding that had recently damaged a good portion of Austin had also washed away many of the colonies when the flood water got too high. And many of the bees died. It was a hardship for Konrad as well because he lost a lot of his honey crop that year. I was so sad; Konrad was, too. He explained to me that bees are fragile, and that was exactly why my mission to help save them was even more important than ever.

I thought very seriously that day of what would happen if we didn't have bees in our world. There was a scene in a documentary I had watched titled *More than Honey* where the director, Markus Imhoof, filmed a group of farmers in northern China dabbing what looked like a cotton ball of pollen by hand onto weakly flowering trees. There was not one single bee in the entire field of trees in bloom. As the documentary went on to explain, it's because there are very few bees left in China. Leaders in the 1950s exterminated the birds, which led to an increase in crop-destroying insects. So they used pesticides to kill the insects, which in turn killed the bees. I couldn't imagine a world without these beautiful creatures, where humans would have to replace them by hand-pollinating flowers and trees. Maybe in the future, large machines would do it.

As we were leaving the farm, I told my parents that I

wanted to start teaching other people about the bees in more detail and not just promote saving them while selling lemonade or through donations. I suppose I had been presenting short talks to store managers about the bees when I went to sell my lemonade, but I hadn't really been doing hands-on presentations.

The next day, I asked my fourth-grade teacher if I could do a presentation about the bees. I had just turned nine years old and felt, after four years of talking about the bees to customers and shop owners, that I was ready to talk to larger groups. She was very encouraging. So I went home and thought about how to display all the information I had gathered over the last couple years and how I would present it in a straightforward, interesting way. I bought a trifold poster board, cut out a bunch of colorful pictures, and designed it to focus on three main topics: "All about the bees," "Why they are dying," and "How we can save them."

I shared my knowledge at my school in front of my classmates, then in other classrooms. Then other schools. I presented at my church, then other churches, then other organizations. This kind of work toward saving the bees became separate from selling lemonade; what was interesting was that my lemonade business became a platform to open more doors to speak about the bees, which in turn supported my company's mission. Having a **business platform** means to take the resources you have built—such as my company, my bottle's label, social media, national television interviews, conferences, my nonprofit—to share ideas and knowledge with as many people as one can reach.

It was fate when, in 2014, my mom and I went to get groceries at a Whole Foods Market near our house and a woman was doing a demonstration on a healthy product. I said to my mom, "I want to do a workshop like that here about the bees!" By coincidence, one of the Whole Foods team leaders had just read about me in the local paper and was eager to have me do a workshop for kids at the store. National Pollinator Week was coming up in early June, I was just about to graduate from the fourth grade, and they were planning a series of Whole Kids events for the summer, and it would be a perfect time to start a bee workshop at the store.

So I did just that.

In every presentation I gave, including the one at Whole Foods, I emphasized that *without bees, our entire food supply will collapse.* I shared the history of bees—that we have relied on them for nine thousand years—and I explained how much we rely on them today: They produce an estimated $15–30 billion in agricultural productivity every year. And one in three bites of food comes from a bee-pollinated plant. I offered the same information to a troop of Girl Scouts.

But it was when I gave direct examples of what the world would look like without bees that I really got people's attention. I would ask people to write down three things they had eaten in the last twenty-four hours. People would write down things like hamburgers, cereal with milk, apple juice, almonds.

"Almonds," I would say. "California is the largest producer of almonds. Typically, their orchards combined take 1.5 million bee colonies to pollinate flowering trees."

"Pizza. There's cheese on your pizza, and cheese is made with milk. Milk is produced by cows, and cows eat alfalfa. What pollinates alfalfa?"

Bees!

Tomatoes, too, are pollinated by bees. In fact, bees are the only insects able to pollinate tomatoes. The flowers of a tomato plant must be vibrated by wind or bees in order to release pollen for fertilization. Even more, the flower must be vibrated at a specific frequency to release the pollen. The honey bees are not able to vibrate the tomato flower in this way, but fortunately, their close cousins the bumblebees and other native species can. So without tomatoes, no pizza sauce, and no pizza.

People were always surprised to learn how much we rely on bees for the food we eat without knowing it.

Within days of my first Whole Foods event, we got a call from the buyer asking if they could carry my product in their store. When my parents told me the news, we quietly squeezed each other's hands. This one was a big celebration, but sometimes big news needs to be approached with careful consideration. We were honored to get the invitation, but we had to ask ourselves if we would be able to fulfill the distribution needs of such a large client. Whole Foods stores see an average of over four thousand shoppers each day.

I closed my eyes and smiled. *Nothing can stop me now*, I thought. Whole Foods was a large stage, and I was going to bring as much attention to the bees as I could.

That night, I sat on my bed processing the news. I was nine years old and about to supply my lemonade to one of the premier grocery stores in the country. I looked at the gold trophy I had won at the Austin Children's Museum when I was six years old for Most Creative Lemonade and remembered all the many lemonade stands and events it took to get to this point.

I was focused on getting my product into as many stores as possible. There were so many things my parents and I were still learning about the beverage industry. We would not just be competing in a highly competitive market for shelf space but competing to *keep* shelf space. More stores, more fees; they would add up quickly. When I asked my dad what it might take to fulfill Whole Foods' needs, he joked, "Survival."

As much as we tried to keep on top of everything before this, our biggest goal now would be just trying to meet production demands.

"Should we take a pass on it, Dad?" I asked, a little nervous for what his answer might be.

"You're going to feel uncertain about business decisions all the time," my dad said. "But . . ." he continued, "I think you're up for the challenge."

"I am!" I said.

"So let's seize this opportunity, even if you don't feel quite ready. I know you, and you'll get ready," he said with a smile.

Sometimes business growth just happens like that; in my mind, there was no other answer but yes. We might not get another opportunity like this.

When the commercial kitchen called to say my shipment was ready to be delivered to Whole Foods, I put on a bright yellow dress to make my first delivery to the store. My brother joked that I looked like I was going on a job interview. In a way, I was. Every time I made a delivery or met with a buyer or manager of a store, I was representing my product, so I always made an extra effort to look my best, and I usually dressed in something yellow—which had become my signature color.

We arrived at the loading dock early that morning with six cases of my lemonade and a pull cart we had borrowed from the copacker. But when I got to the loading dock door and rang the bell, I was told I wasn't allowed in the loading area because I was a minor. I wasn't allowed to unload in the store either. My mom suggested she could deliver the bottles of lemonade, but I wanted to deliver them myself. I must have looked confused and upset because the manager called the buyer and started to speak in whispers.

"Okay, yes, the buyer confirmed you're delivering a product. We'll let you onto the loading dock. But be quick." So off I went, back to the loading dock with my wagon and six cases of lemonade.

As my mom and I started to unpack the wagon, another manager came out and said, "Oh, we only need two cases."

My mom intervened: "Oh, I brought extras in case you wanted more." She continued to unpack. "They run out pretty quickly." She smiled.

"No. Two will be fine."

We were a little disappointed, but two cases were better than none. I gave them an invoice for two cases, leaving a copy for them and taking a signed copy for my files.

Two days later, the Whole Foods manager called and asked for four more cases. A few days after that, five cases, then six. We had sold out quickly before, but this was like nothing we'd ever experienced.

A new Whole Foods was opening in Austin, and they wanted to feature my lemonade. Why? It sold well in the first store. One store quickly became two. Then three.

When I went to deliver my lemonade

I loved delivering my own lemonade

to the newest store the day before it opened, the Whole Foods manager asked me to come inside. He led me and my mom to where my lemonade would be placed. When I got to the beverage aisle, I quickly noticed a huge sign with a picture on it of me holding a bottle of my lemonade. A few weeks earlier, a marketing person from Whole Foods had come by my house to take some photos of me holding my lemonade, but I hadn't thought much of it at the time. Now I knew what it was about.

I asked my mom why she thought my lemonade was doing so well.

"Is it because we followed the 4P's?" I said.

She laughed.

The most commonly used tool in marketing is called the **4P's**. It's when your business considers Price, Product, Promotion, and Place.

THE 4P's

1 **PRICE:** We had started with a base price of $2.25 at East Side Pies, but by the time we got into Whole Foods in 2014, we sold it at $2.50. We had determined the best price point by investigating the premium charged by other types

of beverages, like specially brewed teas and cof-
fees, and considered the prices of other lemonade
products. We balanced this with the amount customers were willing to spend on a product such as
ours and compared this to our production costs to
ensure profit. It was at the right price.

PRODUCT: Early on, we diligently
taste tested and perfected our product.
It was healthy; it was unique. Once we had
our signature recipe, we did not stray from that.
Successful brands tap into the senses to create
memories of the brand image in a buyer's mind.
It's important to remain consistent in flavor.

PROMOTION: I went to as many
events and set up as many lemonade stands
as I could around Austin and surrounding cities
and towns. Plus, I had now incorporated store
demos and workshops into my schedule. My story
about saving the bees through lemonade had
landed some key articles in local newspapers and
television spots.

PLACE: Whole Foods and the other
stores that carried my lemonade all attracted
customers who were looking for healthy food and
beverage alternatives. These were my targeted

customers—people specifically looking for juices made without high fructose corn syrup. It's an important business lesson to consider: Understand who your customers are and where they shop.

"Yes, we followed the 4P's of marketing," my mom said, considering it. "But, honestly, I think you surprise and excite people with your age, your story, and your mission to save the bees."

I'll add one final *P* to the 4P's: *Power*. Never underestimate the power of your story.

Promoting my lemonade stand

Getting ready for farmers market

CHAPTER SEVEN

Austin and Beyond

I learned very
quickly that it's wise to launch
your product in your own backyard, or
in my case, my front yard—but meaning your own city—
because you have to win your city first before you can win
other cities, then other states.

There was a lot of value that came out of building my
business locally, and it's an important lesson for you to
consider when starting your business: *Begin your growth
locally* and take advantage of local resources—it can save
you money, and it feels good to watch your company grow
and touch the people around you.

Almost every aspect of my business had a local component from the very beginning. First, one of the most

Buzziness IDEA

Begin your growth locally and take advantage of local resources— it can save you money, and it feels good to watch your company grow and touch the people around you.

important ingredients in my lemonade, the honey, came from a local vendor, which directly benefited my community's farmers and their bees. My first events and therefore my first customers were local—and became my best taste testers and greatest supporters. My friend's mom who designed our label was local. Austin's local newspapers and television stations supported me. My local commercial kitchen produced and packaged my product. And distribution came in the form of me and my little red collapsible wagon—the benefit of delivering my product myself was that it was a lot cheaper to distribute my lemonade to vendors without having to pay a percentage of the profit to distribution fees, which can add up quickly. I also got to learn a lot about what other business owners were doing in my community—some are now big corporations—that started from the ground up. I was happy to support them as well.

One of the best parts about launching a business locally is connecting with your customers in person. If you are not interacting with people who are potential buyers, introducing yourself, sharing your story, listening to their stories, then you're not making an emotional connection with consumers. Without engaging with the people you wish to

sell your product to, it becomes harder to grow your business and less rewarding. Plus, what I've discovered is everyone has their own bee-sting stories!

Local growth is inspiring, manageable, powerful, and rewarding. With a supportive base at home, I found I had more confidence and experience to go beyond city limits.

When we started to expand beyond Austin in 2014, we were lucky enough to do so within a single network of Whole Foods stores. With three stores in Austin, we headed to Houston. There, we met buyers with just as much enthusiasm for my lemonade. But in Houston, I wasn't a local vendor anymore, I was a "Made in Texas" brand. A **brand** is something businesses use to identify themselves. It can be in the form of a name, slogan, design, color, term, or symbol.

Buzziness IDEA

Local growth is inspiring, manageable, powerful, and rewarding. With a supportive base at home, you have more confidence and experience to go beyond city limits.

I continued to meet with customers in stores, did a lot of presentations and workshops, and increased my product's footprint slowly. With a few stores in Houston, we headed to Dallas. When I entered one of the stores in Dallas, I saw that there was an advertisement of my lemonade on a Whole Foods poster right as you walked in.

"Mom, why are they showcasing my lemonade?"

"Because they love to support and highlight local entrepreneurs."

It was something I hadn't considered, but it's important to remember: Stores and providers of your product want to offer their customers good experiences. Good experiences mean returning customers. Your product is part of a consumer's experience. It speaks for you, but it also speaks for the store. My lemonade told customers it was healthy, delicious, and attached to a mission. I had created my product, but now it was doing the speaking.

As I got into more stores in Houston and Dallas over the next few months, I was growing my brand and building a pipeline. A **pipeline** is the amount of revenue a business expects based on a long period of time between placement of orders. But growing a brand and building a pipeline was costly. Production costs would increase, and distribution from our facility to places outside of Austin would need to be reconsidered as well. We had to discuss these changes with our commercial kitchen. The owner was pleased with our growth but was not enthusiastic about taking on larger orders.

Buzziness IDEA

Stores want to offer their customers good experiences. Good experiences mean returning customers. Your product is part of a consumer's experience.

Our rapid growth had already put a strain on their small kitchen. They had other clients they needed to serve and orders to fill. In the beginning, we were producing small batches using a twenty-five-gallon kettle once or twice a month. Then we moved up to a bigger fifty-gallon kettle every ten days. They would fill bottles using a single-head filler and then cool the bottles immediately in a separate area. Now we were asking for a significant increase in output. Our growth was starting to take time away from their other products.

I didn't want to leave our local copacker; there was a handmade feel to their process. It was a difficult decision, but there was no choice. We had to go.

We found a larger commercial kitchen farther away from us but still in Austin. It was a huge, state-of-the-art facility. They could easily handle our volume, and could

produce much faster. Our lemonade was now made using two-hundred-gallon kettles; they filled twenty-four bottles in a minute with twelve-headed bottle fillers. The speed at which they produced my juice was staggering.

The downside was that we again had to make a few hard decisions to stay within our budget as we grew. Our bulk shipments of lemons were getting costly, so we turned to bottled lemon juice. I had wanted to keep the hand-squeezed component of my product, but at the volume we were producing, it was impossible to sustain; it also saved the business a lot of money without affecting the taste of my lemonade.

The benefit to working with such a large manufacturing facility was that it gave us a chance to focus on organizing our fulfillment and delivery orders, and while it cost more to go to a much bigger commercial kitchen, our bottling and distributing systems became more streamlined and organized.

With several stores in Austin and growth in regions of Texas, we were getting even bigger, which meant I got asked bigger questions. One customer asked, "Do you only have one flavor?"

It was an interesting question. I did only have one flavor, but I guessed I could create more. But what flavors? And how would I even do that?

At that same time, Jacob, who was six then, announced

at the dinner table one evening, "I came up with my own lemonade recipe, and I'm selling it at Austin Lemonade Day!" It was no surprise he had picked up a few business takeaways, since he pretty much grew up watching me start and build a business. He never seemed to mind helping me and my parents at lemonade stands and enjoyed coming to some of my presentations. But I think I learned a lot from Jacob, too. I learned that being a good entrepreneur meant a willingness to teach other people how to start their own businesses and be successful. I had many mentors along the way, and I wanted to be as helpful to others as they were to me.

It turned out Jacob had a pretty smart business plan that he'd been thinking about for Lemonade Day and a product already developed. Since he loved and was inspired by martial arts, he had created a ninja-ade lemonade. One of the ingredients was ginger, so it gave the lemonade a spicy kick. It was quite good!

On Lemonade Day, a few weeks later, he went to South Congress Avenue, one of the busiest, most popular streets in Austin, and was given permission by an Asian restaurant to sell his lemonade in front of their store for the day. He dressed in his martial arts outfit and had his own mission, his own elevator pitch, and his own way of connecting with his customers.

Afterward I asked him if he wanted to do more lemonade stands. He shrugged his shoulders and said, "I dunno. I have a lot of other things I want to do."

"Well," I continued, "I'm thinking of creating more

flavors for my lemonade business, and I like your ginger idea."

"Ninja-ade is awesome!" he said.

"I think you should bottle it," I said with a wink.

"Wanna buy my recipe from me? I'll sell you the trade-mark rights."

I was wrong. My brother hadn't learned *a few* things about running a business, he'd learned *a lot!*

"Buy your lemonade recipe?" I didn't have to think about it too long. "Of course!"

He paused for a moment. "On one condition," he said. "I want to be head of sales in your company."

It was a deal.

Consumers want choices. My one lemonade flavor might be good, but more choices might be better. And yet too many lemonade choices would be bad. So we started researching. I had to anticipate what flavors consumers might enjoy. My concern with creating new flavors was losing the unique taste of my original recipe and then potentially having to add artificial ingredients.

The one thing I absolutely did not want in my beverages was high fructose corn syrup. As you're probably aware, it's an artificial sugar made from corn, and I had read that it's really bad for us and is in everything these days. High fructose corn syrup can be addictive. When we reward ourselves with candy or ice cream, it's part of the brain's reward system circuitry. Yes, that's a real thing. And the problem is too much high fructose corn syrup as part of our regular diet can lead to some pretty bad stuff—like obesity, heart disease, diabetes, and cancer. Over time, it also slows memory in the brain.

I read that our bodies have not yet evolved to process high fructose corn syrup properly. We had been talking about evolution in school and why it was important. Evolution helped to improve the quality of human life. Vestiges were something else we were learning about: those things we didn't need anymore but still had, like tail-bones and wisdom teeth. Then I thought about the bees and how they evolved. I did not want to see our future selves evolve in a way where in the future high fructose corn syrup became normalized and natural sweeteners like honey were not important anymore.

I had become a keen observer of people's habits in grocery stores. I watched particularly how people shopped in the health food aisles. People looked at labels. I thought about how my mom shopped. "I'm not putting this stuff in my body," she'd say. "And I'm certainly not putting it in yours." Then she'd put it back on the shelf. "Anything I can't pronounce doesn't go into our bodies." I wanted people to look at my labels and recognize all the ingredients and feel good about putting them into their bodies.

Developing new flavors of lemonade was growth at what seemed like a good time. I had been selling lemonade for over four years, and we now had a new copacker who had streamlined our fulfillment process and could handle producing more flavors. But I wanted to create new recipes the right way and not rush through the process just to get new products on the shelf.

I expressed this concern to my father. He had a simple answer: We would have to become food scientists. I didn't even know that was a thing. **Food scientists** research and study the chemical changes in both processed and stored foods and beverages. They focus on what chemical reactions occur in foods when they are canned, bottled, stored, frozen, and packaged. There was a lot to being a food scientist.

Here is how a food scientist works: First, you start with a formula and ask what the goal is. In our case, we started with a tinkered version of my great-grandmother's flaxseed lemonade recipe and were looking for other flavors that would taste good without the added sugar, and absolutely no high fructose corn syrup. Then you look at all the ingredients and the chemistry behind the ingredients, like how many calories does each ingredient have and how does sugar react to those other ingredients. Then test to see what happens when you reduce the amount of sugar. Do you lose the sweetness? Can you still keep calories low? A food scientist takes the information, tests products, and reports their findings toward the intended goal.

We focused on using honey as one of the main ingredients to keep it natural. The natural sugars in honey (fructose and glucose) get digested quickly and make it a good natural energy boost. It remains to this day one of the key ingredients in our product. We also learned it paired well with monk fruit as a natural sweetener. It was healthy and complemented the sweetness of the honey. This healthy combination of fruit sugars reduced our reliance on cane sugar.

I'd never heard of monk fruit before. I didn't even remember seeing it in grocery stores. It got its name because centuries ago it was monks who cultivated it, and it's about two hundred times sweeter than table sugar. It has zero calories and carbs, and does not raise a person's blood glucose levels—which was especially important for diabetics. The downside to monk fruit was that it's not grown in the United States, so I definitely wouldn't find it locally. It is only grown in Southeast Asia. The upside was that it's a natural sugar and kept true to our brand's mission of using ingredients that were healthy and natural.

"I don't know what monk fruit is, but at least I can pronounce it," my mother said.

We now had four flavors: the original lemonade with mint, lemonade with ginger, lemonade with iced tea, and lemonade with prickly pear. I was particularly excited by prickly pear. It's found everywhere in Texas. My home is surrounded by prickly pear, so it felt like a real Austin flavor. To be clear, prickly pear isn't a pear, it's a cactus. The juice comes from the one little red fruit at the top of the leaves of the cactus that, when peeled to remove the outer skin of small spines, is delicious.

When my cousins came to visit from New York, they found out how delicious they are, but they also found out just how prickly the spines are as well. They learned the best way to remove the spines from their forearms is by placing packing tape on the arm, then... rip! Ouch.

I was really disappointed when I was told we wouldn't

be using prickly pear from Texas. Surprisingly, there were no organic prickly pear farmers growing cactus in mass quantities in my state at the time. I would have to buy from a farmer in Arizona. "I don't want to sell a Texas-inspired flavor that comes from Arizona," I told my father.

The farmer we chose was a respectable business owner. His farm was sustainable, and he grew his crops with no pesticides. My father reminded me that if I was looking to become a national brand, perhaps it was okay to support a responsible farmer from another state. He had a good point. Plus, I would be introducing people to a fruit found in Texas, which consoled me.

I would describe the flavor to people as a cross between blueberry and apple, but Jacob said it perfectly when he countered, "No, more like bubble gum and watermelon." Yes, that's exactly what prickly pear tastes like.

Jacob was the food critic of the family. Whenever he was trying one of our new formulas, he'd get into his role of food critic and use "the voice." He'd take a sip and say in a refined, manly voice, "Oh, this is a complex flavor profile." Or "I do say, the consistency of this blend is quite good." Or "Mmmm, yes, this one lingers on the palate." He was always right, too! We actually have a whole color/

flavor chart hanging in our small home office that we follow. Like I said, there's a lot that goes into making lemonade.

Now that we had new flavors, we thought it would be a good time to redesign our BeeSweet logo. We worked with an incredible branding firm from Austin called Sanders\Wingo. They put a lot of time and energy into our redesign and loved my mission to save the bees. Because we didn't have much of a budget, they didn't charge us for their services.

As we got more into the process of developing and producing these new flavors, my dad had more conversations with me about keeping costs down. We would need more ingredients with each new flavor; how would that affect our budget, and our profit? But it wasn't just about the ingredients we used; other expenses started to come into question again.

"How do you feel about plastic bottles?" my dad asked me one day. "They're a lot cheaper than glass, and they're lighter, so they cost less to transport."

"Absolutely not," I said. I would not cave on cutting costs by going plastic. Part of my mission as a business owner isn't just saving the bees—it's also being a responsible business owner. I could control whether or not I used glass or plastic. That felt very important to me. So I insisted on not cutting that cost. Glass bottles it was.

Now, at age nine, I was taking my business to a new level. We were starting to produce four flavors of lemonade in no time. Through this transition, we learned a lot about manufacturing. The lesson I took away, as a business owner, is that with growth comes continued learning opportunities in areas you never imagined. I never imagined thinking much about the size of a commercial kitchen's kettle. What was the difference between a twenty-five-gallon kettle and a two-hundred-gallon one besides size? What I learned was that the bigger the kettle, the longer it takes to boil water. And the longer it takes to boil water and heat up the batch, the more flavor you lose through evaporation. Which meant recipes had to be tweaked. But to know just this one detail was all part of the growth experience. It's important to see the entire process as you're growing, because it gives you a bigger picture of how the world works. I now look at food and beverage products differently. I see the science that goes into making all the things we eat and drink. I understand how a few little details can impact an entire business's cost, like distribution channels—one way of loading and shipping my beverage might cost much more or much less than another way. But all of this is critical to embrace and not shy away from. Learn to be present and ask good questions.

CHAPTER EIGHT

From Austin to Hollywood

Early on, when I was still selling my lemonade at a stand in my front yard, I met a woman who would forever change the course of my business. Natalie Cofield was the CEO of the Greater Austin Black Chamber of Commerce. She was good at reaching out to the business leaders of our community and even better at connecting them with big opportunities.

In March 2014, Natalie called me up and said the chamber of commerce was holding auditions for ABC's hit show *Shark Tank*, and was I interested? I was excited, but my parents were concerned and quickly intervened.

"Thank you," my mom said politely, "but we are way too small for *Shark Tank*." Plus, my parents felt the panel of investors that they had seen on television could sometimes be tough on the entrepreneurs who came on the show, and they didn't want to put their nine-year-old daughter through that. Natalie understood.

But the chamber called us again a few weeks later. Again, we declined. A few months went by, and she called again. There was another round of auditions for the show, and Natalie pushed. "You are growing, and it would be nice for you to get some seed money." That part was true. We were growing not just in Austin, but now in other parts of Texas, and entrepreneurs are always looking for investors—especially young start-ups like mine. Whether it's a loan or an investment, it can be hard to find people who have the resources and expertise to help you grow. We hadn't been actively pursuing investors, because we didn't have time, but it did cross our minds. I wanted to be able to produce more lemonade for potential buyers to get into more stores, and we figured $25,000 would have helped make that possible.

Here's how an entrepreneur might look for money.

You start out with the amount of funding you're looking for. So let's say I'm looking for $25,000 to expand my production line.

A business will often go to different people and banks for money to help them build their business. Each time you do this, it's called a **funding round**. The first round of money that you receive is typically called the Friends & Family round because you get the money from, you guessed it, your friends and family. These are the people that invest in you because they know and love you, and they want to support your interest. Depending on how much you need to raise, this is always a challenge. But for a nine-year-old in need of money to grow her lemonade stand, this was especially challenging. For some reason, adults were not immediately interested in turning over large amounts of money to someone still playing with dolls.

The second round of funding is called Angel Investors. These are typically people who enjoy and support different causes and invest to encourage small businesses. Sometimes they contribute millions of dollars to the right company. Again, not many have a history of investing in nine-year-olds. After this, you reach the round of serious investing, the Venture Capitalists. These are really big investors who invest every day as their profession. They typically deal in very large sums of money and scrutinize their investments very carefully. The investors on *Shark Tank* are considered venture capitalists, and Natalie was asking us to bypass two rounds of funding and go straight to the big guys. It would also be very nice to increase my audience through national exposure on television.

Natalie's last call came in just as my mom and I happened to be driving by the chamber's building where the auditions were being held. We took it as a sign of fate, and so we stopped in.

I wasn't prepared at all for the audition. I was wearing my school uniform, and the only promotional materials I had were a small packet of news clippings featuring my product and one bottle of lemonade. (I always carried cold lemonade in a cooler in the car in case there was an opportunity to sell some at a store.) I remember it was a chilly day and late in the afternoon, and I couldn't help but wonder if the judges I was auditioning in front of would be in the mood for lemonade.

When I walked into the chamber, I was immediately greeted by Natalie, a familiar face. But I was going into a room full of strangers, and I didn't feel prepared. I was nervous. My mom called my dad and told him to bring in his laptop, which had a simple marketing video we had created with the help of a friend a couple months earlier. It wasn't great quality, but it would have to do. He rushed through the chamber's door with his laptop moments before I got called in. We queued up the video, and I was sent in to meet with the judges, by myself.

I quickly discovered the panel was very nice. They asked me about myself and then asked about the product, where I produced it, how much it cost. Total revenue thus far. I knew my business inside and out. Being a small business forced me to wear many hats—not just many bee costumes. I had to wear a marketing hat, a financing hat, sales hat, a hat when I was the creative director, a hat when I was focused on my role as a CEO, and of course a hat when I represented the bees.

After I'd answered all their questions, they gave us some additional information and a business card, and we left. I

didn't feel as confident about the interview. In fact, I was pretty sure I blew it. There were several other people auditioning, and they all had scripts and folders full of information about their product. They were all prepared. My dad was not pleased we had decided to do something so last-minute. Plus, he still thought that going on national television was a lot of pressure for a child. But my mom and I weren't too worried. "Oh, we probably won't make it past the first round of interviews anyway." My mom laughed it off.

Buzziness
IDEA

Being a small business will force you to wear many hats—a marketing hat, a financing hat, a sales hat, a creative director hat, a CEO hat, and a hat that represents your mission.

A few weeks later, we got a call from a *Shark Tank* producer asking for us to submit a video saying why I wanted to be on *Shark Tank*. I was very excited! But the producer explained, even at this stage, it was very hard to get on *Shark Tank*. Over thirty-five thousand entrepreneurs applied to get on the show each year, and less than one percent of those actually made it in front of the cameras. And getting a deal with the Sharks was even harder. There were no guarantees.

Still, I wanted to continue, and this time, I wanted to make a professional video. If we were going to do it, we might as well do it the right way. My father finally agreed to go along. After all, it was a once-in-a-lifetime opportunity.

We contacted a local videographer named Justin who had done some work for us in the past, so we knew that he was good.

Justin came by the house with his camera and a few filters. He gave us some prop ideas and placed us in different locations around the house. He shot my mom and dad on bar stools in front of the kitchen. "This is where the magic happens." They smiled and laughed. Then he made it a point to have me in front of the poster of an iconic Austin mural so that the judges would see it and know that we are true Austinites.

We went through a series of questions that the show asked us to respond to. For example, they asked my mom and dad questions like *Why do you want to be on* Shark Tank? *What is it about your product that makes it special? Why do you want to help Mikaila? What are the risks for your business?* Then they asked me about the product, why I wanted to help save the bees. Finally, they asked the standard questions that every business owner should be able to answer about their company: *What does your company do? What's the market opportunity?* At any point in time, always—and I can't stress this enough—always be able to answer these two questions.

As we were ending, Justin saw this little bee statue that we had, and he asked me to do something with it. I had no idea, so I picked up the bee and looked at it, and at the very end of the video, holding a bottle of lemonade in one hand and the bee in the other, I waved the bee in front of the camera and said, "Remember . . . buy a bottle, save a bee." I started to laugh because I thought it was so silly. My parents thought it was cute.

We crossed our fingers and submitted the video to *Shark Tank*.

We knew our chances of actually getting on the show were slim, but we were proud of the hard work we did on the video and were pleased with our submission.

In May 2014, we got a call from the same producer. "We'd like you to come on *Shark Tank*, Mikaila!" I was so excited I could hardly speak. But again my parents stepped in with questions. There would be a lot of paperwork and a few lawyers involved. And I would sign some of my business's rights away. These rights could potentially prevent us from doing other shows or using the brand how we wanted to if the show aired. So we called around to a number of friends to get their advice. Some wondered if the restrictions in the contract paperwork were a problem; others had a few suggestions. Finally we called my great-granny Helen. She said, "Oh, you know I'm so proud of you, no matter what you decide to do. But this is an experience that thousands of people could only hope for, and it's been gifted to you. You have to take advantage of it, if only for the experience."

So we decided to move forward and signed the documents. We called the *Shark Tank* producer and said yes. In September, we would be on our way to Hollywood!

It was exciting to have the opportunity to appear on

Shark Tank, but at the same time, we'd seen the show. There was a lot of secrecy around what happened, both leading up to the show and on the stage. We'd seen multimillion-dollar companies appear on *Shark Tank* and get torn to shreds. While we were psyched to have a chance to visit LA and appear, we knew that it would be a huge disappointment to everyone who helped us along the way if we didn't do well.

That put some pressure on us to really prepare. We had so many people supporting us with time and their expertise, most of which we could never have afforded. We didn't want to let them down. I also didn't want to let the bees down. This was potentially a huge opportunity for me to find funding to grow my business and eventually give more toward saving the bees.

So we got to work studying the show and crafting our story. We had to research every angle and be prepared for any question. The Sharks could be unpredictable. I needed to be prepared for that as well. We knew our numbers and we knew our Sharks:

Mark Cuban, American businessman, inventor, owner of the Dallas Mavericks (my dad really liked that!). Daymond John, founder and CEO of the clothing company FUBU. Barbara Corcoran, founder of the Corcoran Group real estate empire. Kevin O'Leary, co-founder of a software company geared toward family education and entertainment. Lori Greiner, known as being the "Queen of QVC." Robert Herjavec, businessman, inventor, and author. Who, if any, of these Sharks would be interested in investing in a kid selling lemonade? I hoped all of them.

Then we put up a big poster of each Shark on the wall near our side door exit so that we saw each one and spoke to them on more than one occasion. Mark, Daymond, Barbara, Kevin, Lori, and Robert. I remember putting together all those facts like it was yesterday. We also pulled all the information that we could about bees, lemonade, and each ingredient, and we spent hours reviewing the company financials. We were used to holding weekly business meetings, but we stepped it up to a new level. We created five-by-eight-inch cards with all sorts of notes: flaxseed and all its benefits; honey, its ancient history and all of the medicinal and health benefits; lemon juice; lemonade and its Middle Eastern roots; tons of stuff. The study guide we created was amazing.

The research, the cards, the Sharks, it was all fun at first. But it was months before we would actually fly to Los Angeles, California, where the *Shark Tank* studio was located, for the taping. As time went on, I knew (or I thought I knew) that I was ready. But some days, it was like pulling teeth, and I didn't want to think about it. I guess to a nine-year-old, six months seemed like six years. I wanted to do the show already—no more practicing! But I stuck with it, and looking back, I'm glad I put in the hard work it took to prepare for the show.

Between May and September 2014, our kitchen table was one big mountain of index cards. I watched every episode of *Shark Tank*, sometimes more than once. Every question the Sharks ever asked, I had written down. Here are a few of the top questions they asked, and here is how I prepared to answer them:

 What does your company do?
BeeSweet Lemonade is a family-run business that makes natural bottled lemonade. We seek to inspire the community to take action to help secure our food supply by saving one of our most important pollinators—the honey bee. We are fresh-thinking, and we have a purpose that extends beyond the product.

What's unique about the company?
The company was founded by me at four-and-a-half years old while participating in a youth entre-preneur contest. Bringing together my interest in bees and inspired by my great-grandmother's 1940s recipe for flaxseed lemonade, I created a functional beverage that brings together flavorful ingredients that have added health benefits. Plus, it's great tasting and offers a healthier alternative to other beverages.

What big problem does it solve?
BeeSweet Lemonade offers a line of products that utilizes unique, high-quality ingredients that have

added health benefits, such as honey, its primary sweetener, and flaxseed. It solves the concern of having too much sugar in your lemonade. It comes in other flavors: ginger, prickly pear, iced tea. With a variety of flavors, it offers the consumer a healthier beverage alternative, bridging multiple market demographics—parents, children, athletes.

I was good at memorizing; I got even better. The hardest part was creating the perfect pitch. I knew that we wanted the pitch to be around three minutes, not too long, not too short. We had a lot of information to convey in a short period of time—the founder, the company, the ask, the mission, and the product, and most important, why they should invest.

We also needed to end with a "call to action" that would motivate them to invest. We sat down at the kitchen table and put the pieces together, leading with a warm hello, as polite Southerners would. We then introduced ourselves and the ask: *We need an investment.* The Sharks needed to know our lemonade was special and what set us apart. One of the key components of the product was the flaxseed. It's extremely beneficial, and we wanted them to say, *Wow! That's amazing.* We figured that they would pay attention if we shared that early.

I rehearsed it over and over. It began: "When was the last time you tried something so good and refreshing and wondered, 'Could this be good for me?'"

Once I had gotten the pitch and questions and answers

down, then my parents and I had to think about what number we would ask for as an investment. We determined I would ask for $60,000—a reasonable investment for a Shark and a significant amount of funding for my company. Originally we were going to ask for the much smaller sum of $25,000. But just prior to our appearing on the show, Whole Foods informed us that they were going to roll us out into the Southwest region—thirty-four stores in total now! We realized that with the sales increase, the value of the company would also rise. Typically, a company is valued at three times its annual revenue. Some companies, especially beverage companies, can be valued at much higher multiples. We figured that we could get to a large enough revenue figure with the new stores to justify a $600,000 valuation—and 10 percent of $600,000 is $60,000. I had to schedule an extra math session with Mr. Moore at school to understand this complicated equation.

A $60,000 investment would be enough to help us provide two months' worth of product at those stores and do demos. We also knew that we were much too small to ask for a really large sum of money. The relative size of the investment would make it easier for the Sharks to support us. And then, we figured, when we showed how successful we were with the smaller sum of money, we knew they'd be inclined to support us with a larger sum later. In reality, we would need a lot more money to go national with the brand.

Since it was my lemonade company and my idea to be on the show, we decided it would be up to me, not one of my parents, to do the pitch. But then we learned that one of them would need to be onstage with me because of my age. That meant the pitch should include us both, although I would still do most of the talking. As a family we wondered who would go on TV with me, my mom or my dad. At first, we thought it would be my mom, because she is funny and a great storyteller. But my mom thought the better story would come from a daughter and her dad. Since my dad knew the most about the financial and product development side, we thought it was best that he focus on that aspect of the storytelling. I would tell the story of how I got started and talk about the bees in addition to the general business questions. My dad would support me with additional details about the financials as needed.

I was nine years old and starting the fifth grade when I took three days off in early September 2014. It was hard taking time off school, mostly because there was a high level of secrecy surrounding the trip. When people asked where we were traveling, I'd simply say that we were going to meet with a potential partner. The show didn't want people to know the contestants going on *Shark Tank* until it aired. Even my closest friends didn't know where I was going. My parents had told me in the past never to lie, but in this case, lawyers were involved, so I had to think up an excuse as to why I would not be attending classes for a few days...

"A trip out West," I'd say, in a general, casual way.

But when seven-year-old Jacob was asked about it, he would say, "I'm not allowed to tell you where she's going … but you should watch *Shark Tank!*"

My parents and I flew to Los Angeles, and I wanted to go straight to Sony Studios, where *Shark Tank* is filmed. I was dying to see what an actual film studio looked like!

But my mom reminded me we needed to buy things for the set first. So we headed to different stores to buy glass containers, cutting boards, mason jars, crates, and coolers. Then we found a grocery store and bought lemons, ginger, mint, and flaxseeds to set up our display. We'd thought ahead about the prickly pear and had picked those in Austin before we flew out. I carried them in my suitcase. We had shipped lemonade to the studio, but I brought a few extras in my suitcase as well, just in case.

We got to the studios, and the first thing I asked to see was my lemonade stand. Had it made the fourteen-hundred-mile trip from Austin to LA in one piece? My father and I both breathed a sigh of relief when we found it safely tucked away in a dark corner backstage. Before shipping it to the studio, my father and I had fun sprucing up the lemonade stand. It reminded us of how far we'd come.

It was also pretty fun assembling the stand in the studio the day before the filming.

"Still standing!" I said, and gave my father a big hug.

"Yes." He exhaled. "Thank goodness it made the trip."

"Could we have a few lights to set up?" my mom asked a producer.

"No lights. We need everything dark backstage."

They had strict rules about lights and sound, and they took away our cell phones and cameras because there was such secrecy surrounding the filming that they banned anything that might reveal how the show was made. Plus, we were only in a limited part of the studio. The greenroom where I would get ready had my name on it, which made me a little nervous and a lot excited. It felt very real now. In a matter of hours, I would be recording for a national audience.

"How many people watch *Shark Tank*?" I asked a producer.

"Oh, about six million per episode."

I tried to imagine what six million people looked like. It seemed like a lot of people. I shook my head and decided not to think about it.

"Don't look at the cameras, just sell your product and pretend they're not even there," one producer advised.

So that's what I did. I didn't focus on the cameras, the studio, or the show. I just relaxed.

I don't remember this, but my father tells people that when I got to the greenroom at *Shark Tank*, I casually pulled out a book and started to read.

"How old are you?" another producer asked me.

"I'm nine, well, almost ten. My birthday is in a few weeks."

"Well, I hope you get an early birthday gift today!"

Shark Tank was recording its twenty-third episode of season six when I appeared onstage. There were three other companies presenting their products that day: a software company, a video device that allowed people to chat with their pets and dispense treats when they were away, and a clothing line. Because of the pet product, there were a bunch of dogs roaming around backstage, which was fun and lightened the mood. I was the first to go on.

When we stood behind the first set of closed doors, just before our turn, it seemed familiar, having seen the show before. We were told it was time, the doors opened, and we walked out. Surprisingly, I wasn't nervous at all. I was more proud, and the moment seemed a bit magical and unreal. We were going to meet the Sharks. We were actually appearing on one of the most popular TV shows in the world, just because I decided to sell lemonade in a bottle. I thought it was pretty amazing how far one little dream could take not just me, but my family.

As we approached the second set of doors, they automatically opened, and the Sharks were seated right in front of us. My smile broadened. It was surreal being face-to-face with the Sharks. The studio was smaller than I'd imagined it would be, and brighter. And the panel of Sharks, who all seemed so enormous on camera, were just regular people size in person.

I looked to my right and saw our stand, a huge screen with our logo, and the product and ingredients. My mom had done a great job setting it up. I think that the Sharks were a bit surprised to see a little girl in front of them. I don't know that they knew exactly what to expect, but because of the childlike lemonade stand, they must have had an idea.

As we stood in front of the Sharks, I kept thinking, *Did we practice enough, will I get nervous, will my dad get nervous, will we remember our lines?* Then it was time for me to launch into the pitch.

"Hello, Sharks. My name is Mikaila Ulmer . . ." Okay, no mistakes. "And I'm the founder and CEO of BeeSweet Lemonade. Sharks, when was the last time you tried something so good and refreshing and wondered, 'Could this be good for me?' Well, Sharks, guess what—I created a product that's good for you *and* tastes great at the same time!"

No stumbles, pauses, slips of the tongue. I wanted to cheer. About halfway through my talk, I looked at my dad. His turn was coming up. He said his lines—no flubs— and after he was done, I delivered my closing line, and we immediately went to the stand to get the samples to serve.

I ended my pitch by asking the panel of investors, "Which one of you will *bee sweet*, join my team, and help me live my American dream?"

Then I handed out samples while they asked questions. Lori couldn't drink the lemonade because she was allergic to lemons, but was impressed with my professionalism. She again asked my age.

"I'm nine," I said. The panel of investors all gave a chuckle.

Buzziness IDEA

It is important to know your company's story, because a person's background and inspiration can be inspiring for others.

Shark Robert Herjavec wanted to know how long I had been selling lemonade and what were my sales to date. My dad explained that we had been in business for five years and last year's sales were in excess of $25,000.

Kevin O'Leary asked where I was selling my product, and my dad and I told them about our deal with Whole Foods Market. Because of our recent regional expansion with Whole Foods, plus other stores and markets around Austin, my dad could proudly say, "We're in over thirty locations in four cities." The judges were impressed by that.

Mark Cuban was curious about the health benefits of flaxseed and how I incorporated it into my lemonade. I told them it was a trade secret that I would only reveal to the Shark I partnered with. They loved that response and said I had good business acumen.

Daymond John asked what the $60,000 would be used for if I received a deal from one of the Sharks. I explained we had just landed an expansion deal with Whole Foods. It was this deal that I needed funding for. Whole Foods had recently talked with us about wanting to supply our product to the entire Southwest region. This would include stores in Texas, Louisiana, Oklahoma, and Arkansas. I went on to explain that our bottling plant was in Texas but that we envisioned using a larger copacker—ideally manufacturing it ourselves in the future.

Mark Cuban and Kevin O'Leary expressed concern about my being able to balance schoolwork and running a business. Kevin said jokingly, "School's gotta go." I looked at him with a serious expression. Lori started to laugh. More seriously, Kevin talked about my sales and expressed concern over my commitment. The other Sharks looked surprised by this comment. He continued to explain that if he were to go into business with me, he would want a full-time partner, so he was out.

Robert, the next Shark to speak, said the beverage market was too competitive for him to want to invest in someone with very little experience, so he was out, too. I accepted his rejection graciously, but I remember being really nervous that things weren't looking good. For a split second, it crossed my mind while we were recording the show that maybe it was a bad idea for my brand to go on *Shark Tank*. I think my father was thinking the same thing.

Mark Cuban said that our business was a bit too small for him, so he passed as well. Lori's allergy to lemons counted her out.

"One Shark left," said Kevin. Daymond John. Daymond revealed that he was working with a major distributor for a convenience store on the East Coast. He would invest the $60,000 in exchange for 25 percent equity in the business. I thought for a moment, talked it over briefly with my dad, turned back to Daymond, and said, "It's a deal!"

CHAPTER NINE

Life After National Television

I would have to wait to see when my episode of *Shark Tank* aired. We called a few times to understand the exact time frame, but taping producers would respond, "When your episode is scheduled to air, we'll try to let you know." We'll *try* to let you know?

While we waited to hear, we were also warned by many sources that when it did air, we needed to be prepared for large orders and media calls, and to get our website ready for lots of traffic. Too many orders at once often crash websites. But we didn't know if we had one week or six months to get ready. We just tried to keep our website updated with current store information and any news articles that had been run about my business. We had our social media sites updated as well, which contained mostly information about bee conservancy. We made sure our website could handle a larger volume. We prepared press releases. It was a busy time for BeeSweet Lemonade; we tried not to feel overwhelmed, but it was impossible. Then they called. Our show was going to air in three weeks. We felt ready. At least we hoped we were ready.

We wanted to have a really big party like so many other *Shark Tank* contestants do, so we ended up having a viewing party at the offices of Sanders\Wingo, the firm that designed the BeeSweet logo that appeared on the bottles during *Shark Tank*. We also invited friends from school and church and a few small businesses who had helped us along the way.

The night of my *Shark Tank* episode, the first call I got before the show aired was from my great-granny Helen. She said, "I just wanted to let you know, the whole state of South Carolina will be watching my grandbaby tonight!"

I hadn't told anybody how the show turned out . . . Well, maybe a few friends figured it out based on my family's increased activity in the business over the last several months. But I thought I'd done a good job of acting disappointed when I got back from recording the show. I kept them guessing. Still, I think my closest friends knew. Truthfully, it was so hard keeping it a secret, but legally we had to.

When I appeared on the television screen, my friends and family screamed and cheered. My mom started to cry happy tears. My dad beamed with pride. I covered my mouth and laughed. I glanced over at Jacob, and he was covering his mouth and laughing, too. It was wild to see myself on national television. It was even wilder to think that six million other people were watching me.

When Daymond made me an offer, the room erupted with joy. "I knew it!" my friends said, jumping up and down screaming. Almost immediately our social media went crazy! We started to get phone calls within seconds. Thank goodness we'd followed the advice of others and hired someone to handle all of our communications and social media outlets on the spot that night. It made it possible for us to respond to every tweet and Facebook message as they came in. That was very important, and a good lesson: Don't underestimate the importance of personal and quick responses through social media and email. It sends the message that each customer and buyer matters to your business. Several days after our episode aired on *Shark Tank* in 2015, we were inundated by emails and had so much traffic on our website that we were worried it would crash. Fortunately, we had transitioned to a platform that could handle lots of volume ahead of time, and we never had that problem. Calls were coming in late into the night, and everyone was ordering my lemonade. People from who-knows-where were wanting who-knows-what and saying all sorts of things to keep the conversation going. I remember thinking, *I'm really just a lemonade stand.* As much as we felt prepared for the instant attention, we weren't at all prepared.

This could happen with your business as well, and you need to be ready for it by having enough of your product available and a sales force to sell it. It might not be because of *Shark Tank*, but it could come with the endorsement of a well-known person or organization. I've heard that when Oprah Winfrey announces her "favorite things" every year in *Oprah Magazine*, every product she endorses has an "Oprah effect" immediately, where thousands of people will start ordering that product every hour.

Buzziness IDEA

Don't underestimate the importance of personal and quick responses through social media and email. It sends the message that each customer and buyer matters to your business.

We had prepared very big runs of lemonade. We had all four flavors going, and we were ready to meet online and in-store demands, which we did. Everything was happening so quickly. At the same time, the moment the show aired, we called Daymond and asked how he might be able to help us now that it was official. He immediately connected us with his business team and various "handlers," who worked with us on specific documents—including legal and financial ones. They asked us detailed questions and pointed out right away that our current business plan was light on information. We had to beef it up.

After talking with Daymond, my mom, dad, and I decided to put together a more polished business plan for us to present to a whole new set of potential investors. It was incredible to think what three people were able to do with the right guidance from a seasoned businessman and investor. The new business plan was much more detailed than our original one when we started out five years ago, and included several new areas that our old plan left off— mostly because we hadn't been big enough to need them. But now we were.

First, we added a detailed **Company Description**. Your company description should not just tell readers about your business, but it is also the place to boast about your business's strength. Mine provided specific details about BeeSweet's "competitive advantages" and the "strategic locations" where my product was being sold.

Next, we added a **Market Analysis** section. My dad had done research on the beverage market to include the current trends and themes in my industry. Plus, we added details like successful competitors, industry outlook, and target market. This section is a great way for your business to keep on top of what is selling and what you need to do to be a better, stronger company.

Since we'd added flavors, our new business plan now had a section titled **Product Line**. This area shares details about product information and how your products benefit consumers.

We had a more detailed **Marketing and Sales** section, which described our approach to how we planned to attract more customers and build our sales team. We also included a **Funding Request** section, where we outlined our funding needs over the next five years—you'll want to be very specific here; give details about how you will use the funds and what the funding will go toward (salaries, equipment, materials, marketing, etc.).

Finally, we included a **Financial Projections** section. This is important because it shows your readers that your business is established, stable, and successful. In here you'll include *income statements, flow statements* over the last few years, and *balance sheets*. These will help the reader chart the financial story of your business.

When the business plan was done, I couldn't believe how professional it looked. I realized something very important working with Daymond, and it's something you should remember, too: Always treat your business like it's a serious organization. It doesn't matter if you're making $1, $25, or $1,000,000 in revenue. If you're generating profit, you're a business. I thought back on what Mark Cuban had said to me in the show: *You're a little too small for me.* My father would always remind me that the size of our business wasn't what mattered. It was our ability to make a profit and our potential for growth. Not big now, but big someday. Maybe even soon.

Another thing I learned quickly after officially being able to say I partnered with a Shark was the importance of knowing people who can connect you with other people. Because of Daymond's fame and exposure, his team could open doors and introduce us to people we otherwise would not have access to. The minute I said, "I'm with Daymond John," the conversation changed. People listened.

Days after *Shark Tank* aired, I would put in full days at school, then do interviews afterward. It seemed everywhere I went, I saw my name on TV and in newspaper headlines: "Nine-Year-Old Lands Deal on *Shark Tank*" and "Nine-Year-Old Gets $60K *Shark Tank* Investment." It was wild.

Everything was going along really well! What could go wrong?

Well, apparently a lot.

A couple weeks after *Shark Tank* aired, we received a letter in the mail from a law firm. My parents waited until my brother was asleep to call me into the office and explain it to me.

"We have an issue with the name of our company," my father said gently. I was confused. I loved the name BeeSweet Lemonade. What could be the issue with it? I thought it was the best and most perfect name for my business.

"There is a company that has requested we change the name of our business because it is too similar to their name," my father explained. "They either want you to change the name or borrow it. But it could cost millions of dollars to borrow the name."

Wow, I thought. I'd been stung by bees, but I'd never been stung by lawyers.

"Why can't they change their name?"

"Because they were around before we were, they believe they have the right to the name," my father said.

"Why are they doing this to me? I'm only ten years old!"

"Well," he continued, "you can't take it personally. But you do have a decision to make."

But I took it very personally.

When my parents explained that the company had filed a lawsuit against us, I could tell by the looks on my parents' faces that this was serious news. I started to cry. I'd had that name for my lemonade stand since I was four years old.

"If you like," my mother chimed in, "we can fight the lawsuit."

I immediately said, "Yes, I want to fight it. Then would I be able to keep the name?" I asked through tears.

"You might. But it would be a hard fight. They are a very large company, and they had the similar name first. Plus, it will cost a lot of money to go to court, and there's no guarantee we'll win."

To give you an idea of how much it would have cost, an intellectual property attorney my mother contacted started and stopped the phone conversation like this: "I charge eight hundred and twenty dollars an hour. You decide if it's worth fighting this lawsuit."

I didn't want to spend time or money thinking about lawsuits and courtrooms; I wanted to make yummy lemonade. But I was still crying.

A few evenings later, my parents came into my room and said, "I know you don't understand why any of this is happening. But understand this: Sometimes you have to lose the battle to win the war."

"What does that mean?" I asked her.

"It's an idiom. It means sometimes you have to fail in a small way to win big in the long run."

My dad chimed in. "Mikaila, the name of your lemonade isn't what's important. It's about you and your story, and the bees. Do you want to spend your time fighting this, or do you want to spend your time fighting to save the bees?"

Of course we all knew the answer.

I learned two important business takeaways from this experience that go together: First, sometimes it's important to stand up for your rights and what you believe in, even if it costs you money. But second, if it doesn't serve your purpose and it's taking you away from your mission, don't let it distract you.

I was not going to let a name change stop me from my mission: "Let's go save some bees!"

Daymond John didn't seem worried about the name change. He said, "Well, just change the name and relaunch your company!" He suggested we could use this situation to reidentify who we were and make the company even bigger and better. I wasn't sure exactly what that meant at the time, but I would hire people to help me learn.

The next day, we went back to Sanders\Wingo's office to begin the process of brainstorming a new name and logo. Everyone was disappointed because they had just created an incredible design for our company that the

Sharks spoke very highly of and complimented. It was hard to brainstorm; we were all committed to our original name and logo.

Buzziness IDEA

Stand up for your rights and what you believe in, but if it doesn't serve your purpose and takes away from your mission, don't let it distract you.

We were still getting calls from around the country for me to come and speak. Team One in Southern California invited me to participate in their Moonshot speaking series.

Moonshot helps inspire Team One's staff by having people share stories about how they turned ambition into action by not just dreaming about the moon but landing one's moonshot. After the presentation, someone in the audience asked, "What was your biggest challenge in growing the business?" We were embarrassed to share, but we decided to let them know that we had to change our name. Chief Strategy Officer Mark Miller, who loved my mission, said he might be able to help and provided a great inspirational message about branding: "It's not the product you sell but the story you tell." I liked that a lot.

We negotiated a one-year time frame to rebrand our lemonade, but we began right away. We met with Team One in September 2015, and they started the rebranding process in November. First, they presented hundreds of name ideas and logos. We went from five hundred name suggestions down to one hundred names, then to fifty names, ten names, and finally down to a few business names: Feisty Bee Lemonade, Grandma's Lemonade, Bee Buzzing Lemonade, and then there was Me & the Bees. I loved the sound of it. So did my family. It was an easy decision. Me & the Bees it was.

Now that we had a name, the designers got to work designing a new logo. They worked through the holidays, and by January, we had the same business with a new name and look. The graphic was perfect.

In the beginning I was sad to change the name of my company. But when I saw the logo they came up with, it was perfect. "Fresh start!" I said. First, were the cool fonts and colors they used. And I liked the name because it allows everyone who believes in my mission a chance to see themselves as the "Me" in Me & the Bees. It's also a reminder that each one of us plays a vital part of the story and the solution to save the bees.

It also showed the year my company was established, 2009. What year a company is founded is important, especially if you've been around awhile. It tells the consumer that your business is stable and your product is desirable.

But the best part of the new logo was the little bee at the top. If you flip it over, it becomes a heart, and if you take the wings off, it's a drop of honey. Our tagline became "Love. Honey. Bees." I used that as motivation to keep me going and keep us growing.

It didn't matter if I had to change the bottle, the label, and the name of my business. It's still my lemonade company. It changed on the outside, but it didn't change what was inside. So, after months of redesign, BeeSweet Lemonade officially switched to Me & the Bees in 2016. And I learned the very valuable, and in my case actual, lesson of turning lemons into lemonade. I started to think of all the negatives as lemons, because lemons are pretty sour and you can't eat them alone. And the positives became my product, my lemonade.

CHAPTER TEN

A Hive Mentality

By the time I was eleven years old and in the sixth grade, I had been an entrepreneur for six years. I had started a lemonade stand, created an original lemonade recipe, learned how to bottle it, sold my product in thirty-two stores in four states (all in the Southwest region of the United States), mostly in Whole Foods stores, gone on national television, gotten a deal from an investor on *Shark Tank*, been sued, and redesigned and renamed my company. Also by age eleven, I was on track to sell 140,000 bottles of lemonade that year.

One evening I got a call from my grandma. "I just saw you on *Jeopardy!*" she said.

"I'm not on *Jeopardy!*, Grandma." I laughed.

"No, I know that. There was an answer about you on *Jeopardy!*"

After getting $60,000 in capital for her lemonade on this show, a nine-year-old got a bigger deal with Whole Foods.

I looked at my parents. My parents looked at me. I had a question about me on *Jeopardy!* We couldn't believe it! *Jeopardy!* was a show that my grandparents had watched every single evening since I was little, and we always guessed the answers for the questions. I couldn't imagine their surprise when they got to see me as a question!

I might have been doing well in my business and becoming more recognized as a business entrepreneur, but I wasn't even close to being done learning about how to run a beverage company. As I gained notoriety, my parents would remind me that the business was only a reflection of who I was as a person. It reflected my values and my hard work. But there's a difference between the person and what the person does. What decisions you make as an individual are how people will define you, but what you do with those decisions, such as bottling and selling lemonade, is just part of the story—it doesn't define you. *Your business shouldn't define you. You will define your business.*

My father would say, "You're a kid first. The lemonade is your side hustle." He meant that being a child was my number one job; making lemonade was giving me a little extra in life and a lot of extra life experience. It was helping to shape my character. But kid entrepreneurs have other things to think about that adult entrepreneurs don't. School

Buzziness IDEA

Your business shouldn't define you. You will define your business.

always has to come first. Before being able to accept a presentation or meeting, I'd have to conference with my teachers to make sure I wasn't missing any important information, homework, or tests.

Kids also have to wake up really early for school and put in a full day of studying, listening, and participating. Friends also must remain in your life. I'd still find ways to spend time with friends at restaurants and shops, and they continued to be an important part of my life throughout the growth of my company. And don't drop extracurriculars. I would still find time to dance and rock climb and play volleyball. I also continued to be involved in school plays and other after-school activities. Sometimes it was hard to stay balanced and feel normal when so many big changes were happening in my life. But that's exactly why you keep the normal in your life. For balance.

It was a wild feeling when my business entered the national stage. I was expecting growth, but within a year after *Shark Tank*, I would see my company grow by 400 percent. In a way, my lemonade company took on a life of its own. Anyone making a decision to start a company may see similar growth if they keep at it. It will start to take on its own story separate from yours.

But what happens when a business does take on a life of its own? Maybe your business has grown to a point where

Buzziness
IDEA

When you fail, don't punish yourself harshly; learn what you did wrong and try again.

you don't know how to manage it or which way to go. How do you know what to do? My mom always said, "You don't know what you don't know." That's how I was starting to feel after *Shark Tank*: There was still a lot I didn't know about running a business, and I didn't even know what questions to ask about how to grow or manage that growth after national attention. What I did know was that I had to take advantage of the media attention I got on *Shark Tank* before my "fifteen minutes of fame," as they say, were up.

Even though I was working with Daymond's expert business team, once you hit a certain level of growth, in any industry, it gets really complicated and really challenging. The beverage industry was no different. The global beverage market was recently valued at almost $970 billion with a growth rate of 5.8 percent by 2025. That means there are a lot of big beverage companies doing a lot of big business. That also means there's a lot of opportunity for new growth, and for new brands to enter the market—which also means more competition for the little guys like us.

Lemonade drinks alone were in a highly competitive market. There are tons of different brands of lemonade being sold in the US right now, all vying for limited shelf space in grocery stores.

It was one thing to have my bottled lemonade in thirty Whole Foods stores in the Southwest region of the United States; it was another to get it to market in other states around the country. I felt like a little fish in a giant ocean, and I needed to learn how to swim with the big fish before I could jump into expansion and risk losing money or going belly-up altogether. I needed to understand how business leaders ran their companies on a larger scale.

When you think about building your business, you might be focused only on growing in your production output and in revenue. That does outwardly look like a successful business. But in order to have a truly successful organization, you must also consider how you're growing your own community associated with your business.

From the beginning of my journey until this point, I had gotten good at asking for advice. Maybe it was because I was a kid and I had a good excuse to ask a lot of questions. Maybe it was because I was so passionate about my mission and couldn't help but reach out to those who could help me save the bees. But what I quickly realized about asking for help was that I wasn't really asking for help. I was asking to learn: from meeting with beekeepers who taught me about the bees, to talking to local grocery store owners who taught me what brands of bottled beverages sell, to researching copackers who showed me how to bottle and distribute a beverage, and more recently, from getting the advice of lawyers while defending my company's name—and ultimately getting their advice not to pursue a lawsuit—to working with a branding company to redesign my business. Once I saw that asking others wasn't about help but about learning, it became easier to reach out. Not only did I learn the value of asking others about their knowledge, I learned *how* to ask them.

Buzziness
IDEA

When you ask questions, you're not asking for help—you're asking to learn.

It's not always easy for a business entrepreneur to ask for advice. I've talked to other businesspeople who say one of their biggest struggles was seeking the guidance of others in their careers. But if you show the person you're reaching out to that you really want to learn from them, if you are specific with your questions, open to all their suggestions, and show them that you're putting into practice what they've taught you, people will want to share their wisdom. In fact, people appreciate being appreciated. Most take joy in someone's curiosity about their work, so don't be afraid, and go ask questions everywhere. Go learn. People love when you're paying attention.

What I also learned was that it's best to start asking questions within your immediate network first, then branch out. Little steps of learning, as I call it, so that you are better prepared to ask informed questions down the road. For me, when it came to asking how to expand my business the right way, I first asked my parents how they thought we should grow into different regions. Both my

Buzziness IDEA

If you are specific with your questions, open to all their suggestions, and show them that you're putting into practice what they've taught you, people will want to share their wisdom.

parents have business degrees and years of experience in the business world. My dad worked at Dell, the computer company, in business operations and was a whiz at data collecting and research, and my mom owned a marketing firm. I also needed to start with them, because this was a family business and we all made these decisions together. My mom and dad were still working full-time—they called Me & the Bees their "second full-time job." I considered my parents both my business partners and my **mentors**.

A mentor is someone who is more knowledgeable in a particular field, and helps guide someone less experienced and looking to learn more.

Mentorship is very important for entrepreneurs, and a lot of people will tell you that having the right mentors as you grow your business can make all the difference in the world. I felt fortunate to have my parents as my greatest support in what I called my "hive," or my network.

What my parents often told me about their professional experience was that they didn't get to their careers easily. They worked hard and instilled the value of hard work in me. Yet when it came time to focus on growing a beverage business beyond our region and beyond Whole Foods, they were the first to say having a business degree and gaining invaluable work experience in various companies is very different than being out there selling a product and relying on those sales to build a reputation.

When you're out there with a lemonade stand, you really learn the value of a dollar and you see how unexpected costs—such as the gasoline needed for your car to travel to different events and demos at stores, and the expense of making and setting up the demos themselves—start to add up. You learn what you're doing in real time. It's hard to see

Buzziness

IDEA

Mentorship is very important for entrepreneurs, and a lot of people will tell you that having the right mentors as you grow your business can make all the difference in the world.

that from a desk in a classroom or behind a desk at work, because running an actual business can be unpredictable. In that respect, having a business is different from learning business theory. There's a lot of trial and error in business. For example, you can get your product in one store and it may sell really well, but the product might not move in another store in a different region. Why? It might be a question to ask your hive.

When my parents didn't know how to answer my questions like *What should my retail price be?* and *What are the logistics of getting my bottles from a local copacker in Austin to another state halfway across the country?* We reached out beyond our immediate circle to industry professionals who

Buzziness IDEA

You have to go into business with a hive mentality, whether it be collaborating with family members or connecting with people in your community. Be aware of the common interests of others and share knowledge, information, resources, and advice.

had experience growing a beverage product. Those who are local are even better, because they're easier to access and get in front of.

One person we contacted for advice was an expert in the beverage start-up industry named Chris Campbell. He started a small bottled cold-brewed coffee company in Austin called Chameleon Cold-Brew. He first grew his product throughout the region and went on to sell his coffee nationally in such places as Whole Foods, Target, and online at Amazon. He also happened to live in Austin.

He offered me a few pieces of advice. First, I remember him telling me to understand the cost associated with distributing your product and set your suggested retail price. You might be self-distributing today, but you need to understand the cost impact of using a distributor. You can always reduce your price, but it's really difficult to increase your price to cover these fees. Factor these costs in before you submit your price to retailers. This was a critical piece of information that stuck with me. Pricing was critical. We had a premium product; honey is more expensive than most sweeteners. We wanted to sell our product at a fair price since I wanted everyone to have the option of enjoying a healthy lemonade. Setting a fair price is a practice all businesspeople should live by. Even high-quality, organic products like mine don't have to be costly. I knew that we could manage the costs without sacrificing quality and then pass down that savings to customers.

Chris also said that as you grow a business, you'll need to be prepared to hire employees. I wasn't quite at that level yet, but knew it would eventually come. He explained that one of the hardest parts of running a business is managing a team of people. There's been a lot of talk about health care since I started my company. A lot. I wanted a healthier product and I knew that I also wanted to do everything I could to keep my employees healthy. It's important to invest in your people and support the culture you want to create from within your organization. This means make your employees happy by offering them good health-care benefits and a good quality of life. His company is known for having low turnover, and it's because he offers his people support and guidance.

Another important piece of advice he offered was this: *Your company must be rooted in compassion*—for people and for the planet. Empower people, build a community, be honest, be kind. I have kept these words of advice close to my heart as I built my business and thought about my mission.

As you grow your business, the next level of your hive of advisors should be your customers. Don't just consider reaching out by surveys, emails, or reviewing "likes" on

Facebook, but actually connect with the people buying your product. What was their experience like? Did they enjoy drinking my lemonade? Was it too sour, too sweet? I wanted to hear it all. Besides saving the bees, my second favorite aspect of running a company was interacting with consumers. I loved doing demos in stores for that reason. I wanted to learn about what they liked and disliked. I also wanted to educate them about the bees and answer any questions they had. Customers always gave great feedback. They told me what flavors they liked and if they thought the price was fair. And I made sure not only to really listen, but to take notes so I wouldn't forget.

Austin was another piece of my hive. From the very beginning, I looked to my hometown for answers and inspiration. Austin was as much a part of my story as the two bee stings were. As an entrepreneur, you will see that inspiration comes from many places. My city had always been incredibly supportive of me. Known for its business incubators, investors, and progressiveness, Austin couldn't be a more perfect fit for entrepreneurs. In the beginning, the city of Austin and its people supported me, like they do for so many of their local businesses. And they have continued to support me. Make sure you reach out and explore locally when you begin to grow. Some of your best resources are right in front of you—and you immediately have something in common: the place where you live!

One thing I learned from living in Austin is how a person's surroundings can affect them. Austin inspired me in every way. Take note of what influences you in your town or city. Even in my small little community of South Austin, I soaked in my surroundings without knowing it. There's our church, Greater Mt. Zion Church, and my church family, which taught me the importance of community. There was the music scene of Austin that has shown me how to express myself and embrace creativity. The food scene, which impressed upon me the importance of quality ingredients and healthy eating and drinking. Even the buildings of the city and the new modern homes being constructed have given me opportunities to understand smart development and smart growth, whether I was aware of it or not. All around me I experienced a sense of vitality. People embraced their ideas and encouraged others to do the same. I was part of Austin, and Austin was part of me.

There was something else in Austin that inspired me as I considered not just growing my business, but respecting and saving the bees: Lady Bird Johnson Wildflower Center. Lady Bird Johnson was the First Lady of the thirty-sixth president, Lyndon B. Johnson. She was an early advocate for preserving the environment with a focus on native wildflowers. She once said, "The environment is where we all meet; where we all have a mutual interest; it is the one thing all of us share."

The center, a short distance from my house, is huge: 284 acres, with more than 970 species of Texas native plants and 70 species of Texas trees. I went there often. The flowers were beautiful, but I went there to study the bees.

Flowers are important to our ecosystem

I couldn't really think about the bees without considering the entire ecosystem. Flowers relied on animals as much as the animals relied on the flowers. I studied the bees and the butterflies out in nature. But I also noticed the foxes and the owls and the grackle birds that squawked and sounded like video games in our neighborhood. And when jasmine was in full bloom, my neighborhood was shrouded in its lovely scent that attracted all sorts of creatures.

In our yard, we created an oasis for the bees by planting flowers and pecan and loquat trees. Even the squirrels that tore up our outdoor furniture every year and used the stuffing to build their nests were a welcome part of the ecosystem. They were important for their seed collection and dispersal. Once in a while, roadrunners appeared in random locations around town. That was my Austin, and it was part of my hive.

As my company grew, one of the most common questions people asked me was *Is it hard to run a family business?* Truthfully, having my company be a family business was the true essence of my hive. But it can have its challenges if you don't draw boundaries. We drew our boundaries right away. If we didn't, we'd be eating, sleeping, and drinking the bees! No business talk during breakfast or at dinnertime. Those hours were strictly dedicated to family time. We also had defined duties in the business. My mom did the marketing and PR; my dad helped with operations and finance; my older brother, Khalil, who was in college at the time, was the IT guru, so he helped with all the tech stuff; and Jacob was the photographer—we used a lot of his photos on social media. He was also our loudest salesperson and biggest fan.

When people wondered about working as a family,

I said it was the best part about the business. Knowing that we were all doing it together and that we loved and supported each other hadn't just allowed the business to grow, but allowed us to grow together as a family.

Another thing I realized about working with my family members was that they kept me real. If I did something without fully thinking it through, they would let me know it. I didn't want to disappoint them or let them down by taking anything lightly. We relied on each other for the business's success. And when sales were lower than projected, or if there was a financial setback, they were there for me, too. My parents often reminded me of the quote in I Corinthians 4:8, "Everything you need you already have." It's a great way to look at life. When things were difficult—and there will always be ups and downs with any business—I reminded myself that I had everything I needed: a great family, a great life in Austin, and a great hive.

Any good CEO and entrepreneur will tell you that you have to go into business with a hive mentality, whether it be collaborating with family members or connecting with people in your community. This means you have to be aware of the common interests of others and think as a community would think, share knowledge, information, resources, and advice. I mean, why not? It isn't easy running a business, and you can't know everything, so let your whole hive shine.

With a hive supporting me, I was ready for what was next.

CHAPTER ELEVEN

From Shark Tank to the White House

As time went by, I started doing more and more presentations on how I started my company and about my mission to save the bees. With each presentation, I learned new skills and became more confident. Here are the five big lessons I've learned for giving a good presentation:

1. Speak clearly and slowly.
2. Use props and your product to make your talk more visually interesting.
3. Avoid using "um" and "like."
4. Don't fidget.
5. Practice, practice, practice!

After my presentations, many people would approach me to let me know how inspired they were or how much they learned from watching my presentation. At the time, I mainly just presented to those who had emailed me. We were getting messages from students, teachers, business leaders, and community leaders. Invitations to speak at various events were coming in from around the world, and I enjoyed teaching others about the bees, our ecosystem, entrepreneurship, and how to start a company with a mission. But it was difficult to read all the emails that were coming in and respond in time. I started to wonder if there was a way for us to make it easier for people to request hiring me for public speaking engagements, and for us to respond quickly. After doing some research, my mom created a form page on our website where people could submit the location, budget, and topics of a presentation.

I was so excited as the requests came rolling in. Some I had to decline because of an important test or assignment, but others I got to accept! With each presentation my love for travel and being able to network with new people grew. When I returned from those trips, I always shared the details with my classmates, and I always looked forward to my next!

In July 2015, I was ten years old and staying at my grandparents' house in North Carolina for the summer when I got a call from my mom.

"Mikaila! You're never going to believe this!" I could tell she was dancing around the living room. "Guess who just emailed us!" She started to giggle.

"Mom, tell me!" I said. I loved when my mom acted like a kid.

"Michelle Obama's team!" my mom said, laughing, and clearly she was jumping up and down.

"What? Who?" I couldn't believe it.

"It says from the Office of the First Lady . . ." She was reading and still dancing.

The email said Michelle Obama's team had heard about my contributions to Texas and they wanted to invite me to the Kids' State Dinner. I didn't know what the Kids' State Dinner was, so I looked it up online. It was a White House event sponsored by Michelle Obama, which gathered and honored fifty kids from fifty states who were bringing health awareness to other kids around the country. Because my lemonade was a healthy alternative to sugary soft drinks, I was going to be given an opportunity to talk with other kids around the country about what they were doing, and I could share my lemonade story and, more importantly, my mission to save the bees.

"You're going to the White House!"

The White House!

I knew that the Obamas cared about the bees. I had read that when they moved into the White House after taking office, they created their own garden, complete with a bee colony. They even had a beekeeper named Charlie Brandts who took care of the bee colony. And a month before I received the call from First Lady Michelle Obama, I learned that President Obama issued a Presidential Memorandum creating a task force to oversee a "Strategy to Promote the Health of Honey Bees and Other Pollinators." Their strategy would focus on three main goals[1]: 1) to focus on the increasing honey bee colonies, 2) to restore the population of monarch butterflies, which were also in decline, and 3) to protect millions of acres of both public and private land that could be used for pollinators.

I was four years old when Barack Obama was elected president. I'd looked up to President Obama and First Lady Michelle Obama my whole life. Mrs. Obama had always been a role model for me because she was a good mother to two strong girls, and she was also a hardworking First Lady who supported the rights and accomplishments of young women all over the world. When I learned they were as interested in saving the bees as I was, my admiration for them grew.

I could see my future self standing in front of a room of reporters, an American flag behind me, cameras in front of me snapping pictures of me looking very presidential. I would be explaining to the world why we needed to save the bees. Mrs. Obama would be standing next to me, nodding in agreement.

"Mikaila, you need to pack your bags. And bring a dress!"

Then I realized something. I didn't have a dress! I was at my grandparents' house with only jean shorts and flip-flops.

---

[1] https://obamawhitehouse.archives.gov/blog/2015/05/19/announcing-new-steps-promote-pollinator-health

But it didn't matter anyway—I had just gone through a growth spurt, and all my dresses at home were a size too small. My mom and I had been meaning to go shopping, but we were too busy. I started to get nervous. I couldn't wear a dress that was too small on me to the White House! There wasn't much time, so my mom just ordered a few new dresses online, and we hoped one would fit. A couple dresses were yellow; some had flowers; one was white. I loved yellow because lemons are yellow and it put some of my brand into what I wore.

"I'll FedEx them to our hotel in DC."

I would fly directly from North Carolina to Washington, DC, on a plane by myself. After I passed through security, I was taken by an escort who helped make sure children unaccompanied by an adult got onto their flights safely. The flight attendant made sure I got a seat near the front of the plane. Just before the airplane took off, one of the flight attendants made an announcement. "We have a very special person on board with us today." I got so excited. I'd always wanted to meet a celebrity. Who could it be? Maybe they were flying to meet the First Lady, too. "She's ten-year-old Mikaila, and she's going to the White House today!" I was pretty sure either my grandma or my mom had something to do with this. They were both good at telling everyone about my lemonade business. All the passengers started to clap. They were clapping for me! The flight attendant made me stand up, and I took a bow. *Hmmm*, I thought, *this attention feels pretty good.*

I met my mom at the airport, and we went directly to

the hotel. I was so nervous about the dresses not fitting me. When we got to the hotel room, there were the dresses laid out on my bed. They were all different styles. All of them but one were too small on me. The fifth and final one I tried on fit, but barely. *Phew*, I thought. It also happened to be yellow—my signature color. But I mixed it up a little and went with a white flower headband, which I thought was a nice touch. I was ready to meet Mrs. Obama.

I stood in front of the mirror and thought, *How could I have grown so much?* I still felt like the little girl who started a lemonade stand in her front yard six years ago. How was it possible that two little bee stings and a lemonade stand got me to this point? Was it really happening that I was going to the White House to meet the First Lady? I had to pinch myself several times that day.

In photographs, the White House looks like a small mansion. But in real life, it's an enormous mansion. It has 35 bathrooms, 8 staircases, 3 elevators, and 28 fireplaces. It takes 570 gallons of paint to cover the outside of the building.

There were several security checkpoints that people had to go through before entering the building. Security guards were polite but serious.

When I entered the Grand Foyer, I was immediately taken aback by the elegance of everything: the furniture and wallpaper, chandeliers and artwork and shiny floors. And I couldn't help but notice how colorful all the rooms were. The bees would have loved the huge fresh flower arrangements everywhere. I imagined them dancing and floating through every room like I was dancing and floating in my mind. Each room was a different color with large and small pieces of artwork on every wall. There were portraits of presidents and first ladies and artifacts collected by Meriwether Lewis and William Clark on their expedition to the west. In one room there was a clock made of all gold, and in another there was a piano held up by three large gilded eagle-shaped legs.

I met up with a group of kids who had also been invited to the State Dinner, and we were given a tour, then we were led to the East Room, which is one of the main reception rooms in the White House, used for large gatherings. When we got inside, there was a military band playing to greet us! The tables were beautifully set for a meal with fruit and vegetable topiaries as centerpieces. I'd never seen anything like it in my whole entire life. There were grapes and tomatoes and Brussels sprouts and strawberries all made into sculptures.

Once we were seated, Mrs. Obama entered at the front of the room and spoke about how thrilled she was to be in the presence of so many young, healthy chefs. She reminded us of how important our role is, because making healthy meals and drinks is the kind of fuel our bodies need to keep moving. Then the room exploded with applause, and I noticed President Barack Obama had entered the room from a side door. I couldn't help but cheer loudly, too. I was in the same room as both the first lady and the president of the United

States! He cracked a joke about his favorite vegetable being broccoli and that maybe that wasn't a very popular vegetable for most people. Then he went around the room talking to kids. Finally, he got to me, and I introduced myself and gave him a firm handshake. It was an incredible moment. Soon after, Mrs. Obama came around the room as we were all in groups talking. She walked toward me and said, "Oh, Mikaila! I know you! Come here." She must have had information on all the kids that day—with photos and all of our stories—but I thought it was so neat she greeted me that way. Then she said, "Thank you for all the hard work you're doing with the bees," and gave me a great big hug.

I remember thinking her perfume smelled like a combination of importance and flowers. She was instantly warm and likable, and she listened to all of our stories with interest and humor. Some kids told stories to her and at times blushed and giggled. But she made us all feel special and comfortable. I thought that was a great quality in a person. I noted it: *Make people feel special and comfortable.* I also noted something else, and it is an important skill for not just entrepreneurs, but for everyone: *Remember people's names.* I know it seems like a minor thing, but it's actually a very important skill to have. I thought, *If the First Lady of the United States of America can remember my name, I can certainly make an effort to remember more people's names.* I'm still working on that one. Mrs. Obama has twenty-seven million followers on Instagram, and she remembered my name. Wow. That's a talent.

The event was a good opportunity for me to tell a larger audience about how the bees are dying and why and how we can save them. How we *must* save them. It's a day I will never forget.

Buzziness
IDEA
Remember people's names. I know it seems like a minor thing, but it's actually a very important skill to have.

I thought that was going to be a once-in-a-lifetime opportunity to be at the White House and meet President Barack and First Lady Michelle Obama, but I ended up getting another invitation to the White House the following year, in 2016, to serve lemonade and Popsicles to over five thousand people alongside several celebrity chefs at the White House's annual Easter Egg Roll.

The tradition of the annual Easter Egg Roll started back in 1878 when Rutherford B. Hayes was president. One Easter, a group of bold children asked the White House guards at the main gate if they could use the lawn to play egg-rolling games. The guards resisted at first, until President Hayes told them to let the kids in. The event has been around ever since.

Thousands of people gathered on the South Lawn of the White House to participate in various games. President Barack and First Lady Michelle Obama greeted visitors and took photographs. When my family and I were standing in line to meet them, we noticed a very tall man in front of us.

"Look who that is!" Jacob said in a not-so-subtle voice. "It's Shaquille O'Neal!" The former NBA basketball star was there to play basketball with a group of young kids. We got to meet him and watched a great pickup game between him and the president. But the best part was, I got to serve the five thousand guests my lemonade, including the president and the first lady.

Jacob and I were given gifts, too: presidential eggs that had a picture of a bunny on the front, the White House on the back, and President Obama's signature on the side.

I keep that Easter egg out all year round as a reminder of something that is important for you to remember as well: When you dream big, like starting a business from the ground up, your rewards are big, too. I had never in my lifetime imagined I'd meet the first lady and the president, or tour the White House, or serve guests my lemonade on the famous South Lawn. But it's only because I had a dream and didn't let go of that dream that I was given those opportunities.

I saw the president once more at the 2016 United State of Women Summit. It was the first summit of its kind sponsored by the president, and I was invited. Guests got nominated to attend and speak, but apparently the organizers had a tough time figuring out what my role would be at the conference—it had changed a couple times. Eventually, after the third call, they decided the best role for me was to introduce the president.

When I got to the podium to introduce the president to five thousand people, I had to stand on my tiptoes. Afterward, he said, "I'll be back on the job market in seven months, so I hope she's hiring." Everyone laughed, and it was an incredible feeling! Then he said someone asked him backstage if I was going to feel nervous speaking in front of so many people, and he said, "No, she said she'd just spoken to eleven thousand last week."

It was true. Only a week before, I had spoken at a large event, and I was not only getting used to speaking in front of large crowds, I was starting to really enjoy it. Because every time I went out on that stage, I thought about sharing my message of the bees with more and more people.

People would ask me if I got nervous speaking in front of so many people. Yes, of course I did! But I would tell them that being nervous means you care about something.

Buzziness IDEA

You might get nervous speaking in front of people, but being nervous means you care about something.

And the more nervous you are, the more you're passionate or excited about what you're about to do. What I was doing had wings, and I could feel the momentum building.

When we returned home from the White House, it was back to normal life, if that was possible. My mother told me not to let all these fancy trips to the White House go to my head. I said I wouldn't. Then with a smile, I said, "You know, President Obama and I know each other well enough now that we do a fist bump."

"Yeah, right. You never fist-bumped the president," my mom said with a laugh.

A week later, an email arrived from Valerie Jarrett, one of President Obama's senior advisors, with a quick thank-you and a few photos.

Jacob said, "Looks like a fist bump to me."

"Ohh... I guess it's true," my mom said, laughing.

With Valerie Jarrett

Meeting President Obama

CHAPTER TWELVE

Growing Pains

Between 2015 and
2017, my story appeared on national television
more than any other time in my company's history. One
thing is for sure, national attention was very good for Me
& the Bees—especially since we never paid for advertising
because we couldn't afford it—and it was good for the bees,
too. People seemed drawn to my story and the work I was
doing because of the bees; plus, everyone likes to see a kid
excited to share their story. Starting a business is tough,
and many people are afraid to even pursue it. A lot of producers and editors believed that hearing a kid tell a story
about starting a business from scratch and passionately
pursuing an interest that benefits us all was inspirational.

Buzziness

IDEA

Identify your strengths, whether it's public speaking, selling your product, creating a solid marketing plan, or inventing new products. Embrace what you are good at and own it!

It was for sure an interesting story. So people were coming to us because we had a social impact. Just in 2015, my story appeared on *20/20*, *The Real*, the History Channel, *ABC News*, *World News Tonight*, *CBS News*, *USA Today*, *Huffington Post*, and more.

I was eleven years old and in the sixth grade when I was invited to do an interview on *Good Morning America*. I remember sitting in ABC's greenroom, and Robin Roberts's makeup artist was doing my makeup. I was about to go on live national television, but all I could think about was how exciting it was that my dad was letting me wear lipstick—it was actually just clear lip gloss, but still. "Just this once," he said with a wink and a hug.

It always surprised people to learn that I didn't really get nervous speaking in front of a crowd or on television. When I was younger I did, but as I got older, I became used to—and even enjoyed—that aspect of founding a business. I would say public speaking is one of my strengths. As a business owner, you will need to identify your strengths as well: whether it's public speaking, selling your product, creating a solid marketing plan, or inventing new products. Embrace what you are good at and own it!

Robin Roberts came to my dressing room and made me

feel even more comfort-
able before we went
into the studio to tape
the show. She said,
"Let's go serve some
lemonade," so we
walked down the hall
of ABC's offices with
a cart and handed
out lemonade to staff
members. Then we
went outside the
studio and handed out lemon-

Meeting Robin Roberts

ade to fans watching the show. I was completely relaxed
and enjoying myself once she started interviewing me.

With all this national attention, people and companies
were starting to approach us with opportunities. At one
point it felt like there were hundreds of opportunities that
would take me and my company in different directions. We
even got an offer to do a reality television show ... I'm still
interested in that! (My parents are not so enthusiastic.) It felt
overwhelming. My parents did not sleep much. Investors
would call offering to purchase our business. People were
selling preservatives that would make our juice last longer.
Distributors called from China. A few people called to tell us
their stories of rapid growth—they knew what it was like to
be in our shoes, that all the decisions one had to make were
stressful.

Because of all the attention, we had to make decisions quickly. People would say fame is fleeting. My mission to save the bees might be trending one week and then gone the next. So we felt like we needed to act. If we were going to market ourselves as a national brand on national television, then we had to act like a national brand—and at that point, we were pretty much just a Texas lemonade company in a few stores in four other states.

We had reached out through our hive network for advice on how to grow. There are several ways to grow and expand as a company, and as you grow, you, too, will have to figure out what strategy is best for you. Businesses have to decide if they want to grow in width or depth first. You might hear that a lot in this stage of development: the **width versus depth** decision. Here is an example of what that means. Let's say you have ten bottles of lemonade. Do you want to set up one lemonade stand and sell all ten

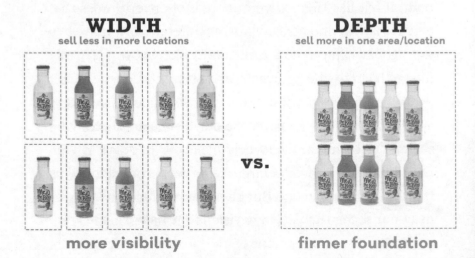

WIDTH
sell less in more locations

vs.

DEPTH
sell more in one area/location

more visibility

firmer foundation

bottles at that one location? That would be depth. Or do you want to set up ten lemonade stands and sell one bottle at each location for exposure? That would be width. Depth means you establish a firm foundation for your business by increasing the velocity and volume of sales in the current store or stores you're in. Width means you're selling in more locations for visibility of product, but you're not selling at the same volume as you would be in one store. You're producing the same volume overall, but distributing it using a different business strategy.

Going deeper first when you're growing a business like mine is the more common and wiser approach because it cuts down on expenses and is less risky. But because media coverage was at the national level for Me & the Bees, we wanted to take advantage of it. Many small companies don't get this opportunity and are limited to focusing on depth. We wanted to be in as many stores as possible so that we could reach the highest number of customers we could across the country. We also wanted the story about the bees to be everywhere immediately. We would focus on depth once we got in the stores.

People were asking for our lemonade after each appearance on a television show, and we weren't on the shelves yet—so we went with width. Width would give us the highest level of awareness for our product and our cause in the fastest way. But branching out to many stores in many states was always risky, and more costly. You needed more management of the product, which meant we would need to grow our staff quickly. Buyers were calling us from as close as Corpus Christi, Texas, to as far as Coos Bay, Oregon, but getting the product into several physical locations at once and on a regular schedule was a whole different beast.

During that crazy time of the meteoric rise of our brand, my mom would say, "We're building a ship while sailing it." It was the perfect way to describe how we felt. We were going fast without much time to process or think through all of our decisions. We made mistakes along the way, but we didn't even have time to process the mistakes because of the speed at which we were growing.

As we were learning the wrongs, we were also learning the rights: There's a combination of the right kind of awareness, the right kind of buyer, the right kind of salesperson, the right kind of selling season, the right kind of pricing. That is to say, we knew our brand and its mission, we knew the kinds of stores our customers shopped at (such as health food stores), we knew what a fair price was for our lemonade, and we knew people drank more lemonade when it was hot outside.

But growth also meant it was time to say goodbye to something special in our lives: our home office. Our home office was a cozy and wonderful spot in a room next to our kitchen, but it was too small. The search began for a place that was in our budget but still allowed us room to grow. Finally we found a space a few miles from our home and right near my school, which was perfect for both me and my parents. It was a big investment, but we all realized the advantages of having a headquarters, or hive, for the company. The office was located on a street named Bee Cave Road, which I loved. I also liked how professional the building looked from the outside.

The first time I stepped inside our new office space, I thought, *Wow, it's huge!* But it was also bare and dreary. The paint was dingy, and the carpeting was dirty, and it had a funky smell. It was just one big featureless room with no personality or inspiration. I didn't want to make a big deal of it, so I smiled and said, "It'll work."

Somehow a company called Varidesk got in touch with my mom and said they'd heard our story and how we'd rented our first real office. They offered to do a makeover if they could film it. My mother agreed. I knew nothing about this. One day I came home from school, and my mom said, "I need to grab something at the office. Will you come with me?" I did.

When she opened the door, my family was there, and the people who did the makeover were there smiling and filming my reaction. The office was gorgeous! Bright and freshly painted! New tables and furniture, and these neat stand-up desks. I couldn't believe it. We had offices!

Having an office was a dream. It allowed us to host meetings, store all our files in one place, and keep work separate from family life. But now we had a lot of empty work desks and we needed to hire employees.

First, my mom decided to quit her job to take on Me & the Bees full-time. Then we also hired a full-time administrative assistant to sort out all the opportunities and keep things in order, and then we found a part-time marketing person.

We also knew we needed to hire a professional sales team to sell our product in more stores. You can only bootstrap it for so long before you need to get the experts to come in and help. We could not do it alone anymore. It was not sustainable. There were many types of services you could use that contracted whole sales teams, which meant they weren't full-time employees for us and handled other businesses' sales accounts as well. It was a perfect option for us. Once we brought in the right sales team, things really picked up. So then we hired a full-time accountant to manage invoices and bills. With increased sales came increased operations. **Operations** was quite a lot of work to keep track of, so we hired an **operations team**, which was one of the smartest things we did; they ended up doing a lot of work for us behind the scenes. Operations means anything that has to do with a company to keep it running and earn money, such as systems, equipment, people, and product. An operations team manages how a business works internally by focusing on its effectiveness and efficiency.

It was a good thing we hired when we did, too, because within one week of hiring our operations team, we got a call from the recall department at one of our biggest customers' distribution centers. I started to worry; no one in the food and beverage industry ever wants to get a message from the recall department. A **recall** is what happens when a product is faulty. Basically, someone was concerned about the quality of our product. We didn't have time to focus on a recall, nor could we afford it. Our operations team took over immediately, and the complaint turned out not to be on our end—it was an issue with the warehouse on the store's side. They had had an unusual freeze in their storage facility, and all the tops of our lemonade bottles had popped off. Having the right people in place saved us many times.

With increased sales came big decisions. What were our new sales goals? We consulted with several experts within our hive, including Shark Daymond, who agreed that with a sales force in place, it was the right time to push growth. We determined we wanted to take the business to new levels of expansion and set our goal of quadrupling sales annually. This was a sizeable increase.

With growth came growing pains. When you grow, everything needs to grow, not just a sales team and more employees, but more technology for the company, more marketing, a larger production line, and a larger distribution force. But none of that is possible without a growth in costs. We would be competing with major beverage manufacturers that had way bigger budgets, way more experience, and way more brand loyalty.

Me & the Bees was officially **scaling**. That means to grow your business while still controlling costs. When you're scaling, you have to be aware of how quickly you're expanding—too quickly and your expenses could go beyond your budget, which would be a problem. But expanding too slowly could also leave you with missed opportunities.

I realized I had been experiencing small points of scaling all along. When I was really young and upgraded from a handheld juicer to an electric one, I guess that was my first scale. Then there was when I was nine years old and decided it would be more efficient to purchase already-squeezed lemon juice for my lemonade. My first big scale was when I got the contract to supply Whole Foods Market. That's when I really had to focus on how to produce lemonade faster in the most cost-effective way yet still turn out a high-quality product. Now, when I was twelve, and in the seventh grade, we were producing thousands of gallons of lemonade at a time.

We had outgrown our local copacker and a second copacker. We finally found the right fit with a copacking facility in Virginia. This copacker was much larger and could service all our needs, plus it was more centrally located in an area where we were seeing a lot of growth. This kept some of our delivery costs down. We also got a new distributor—Rhode Island–based United Natural Foods Inc., one of the largest distributors of national and organic foods. They could handle larger runs all over the country.

But all these new changes cost money. And the return on sales isn't as much as people think. A quick breakdown of profit looks something like this:

When you get a beverage into a store, you should get somewhere between 47 and 65 percent of the price of the product—half to you as profit, the other half to cover

production costs. The distributor, freight company, and retail split a percentage of the rest.

Then there's always a chance something goes wrong, like bottles break or are not stored in the right conditions. In one case, a supermarket left our lemonade out in the sun and rain for several days, and the bottle tops popped off. We had already paid a **slotting fee**. A slotting fee is kind of like renting out shelf space in a supermarket. So not only did we lose money on the production of the lemonade and the freight, but we lost money on a slotting fee and made no revenue, and the store would not refund us.

Buzziness
IDEA
Be aware of how quickly you're expanding when you scale—too quickly could go beyond your budget; too slowly could leave you with missed opportunities.

I found myself inspecting the way my lemonade was being displayed in more and more stores. One time I went into a local store just to see how my bottles looked in the case, and they were selling them for four dollars. We can suggest the cost of our lemonade, but stores can determine their own price.

"Mom, look!" I was shocked.

"Oh, that's ridiculous," she said.

We went to the store manager and asked if they could check to see if it was the right price.

The manager checked and said, "You're right," and corrected the price to a lower amount.

Another local store I visited wasn't stocking enough, so there were only a couple bottles pushed way to the back of the shelf. I had to explain that they needed to keep ordering to fill the shelf. I couldn't go to every store, especially those that were far away. We were advised to hire a team of **brokers**. Brokers go into stores and make sure the product is doing well on the shelves.

It was the hiring of all these separate teams—sales, operations, brokers, plus those who worked in the Me & the Bees office in Austin—that really let me see my hard work paying off. I now had a bigger team of people working with me to help save the bees. It was amazing to see our company grow from my family to a hive of employees. The feeling of having a large team of people all working toward my mission is the most unbelievable and most rewarding feeling I've ever had.

CHAPTER THIRTEEN

Traveling with the Bees

In 2016, the
summer before I entered
seventh grade, I got invited to Cape Town,
South Africa, to participate in a summit hosted by the Dell
Women's Entrepreneur Network (DWEN). The theme of
that year's conference was "Innovate for a Future-Ready
World," and in attendance would be female business leaders from all over the world. It was an invitation-only, two-
day event, and I was specifically asked to teach a course for
the Girls Track program that ran on the same days as the
main agenda.

The DWEN Girls Track was created to give girls
between the ages of eleven and seventeen the opportunity
to work with young entrepreneurs like me and learn from

our experiences. The cool thing about Girls Track is wherever the event was being held, Dell would organize events in that area, and both DWEN and Girls Track would get together and give back to the community. In Cape Town, we partnered with a local organization called Christel House that provided education for girls and focused on health care, character building, and career and family planning. Many of the girls I would be speaking to came from financially challenged sections of South Africa and were selected by Christel House to help put them on a path for success. While other participants came from different parts of the world, all of them were there to learn about female entrepreneurship.

"What are you going to talk about in South Africa?" my mom asked.

I wasn't quite sure. There were so many topics to cover. I had read that other participants at the summit were going to teach girls things like web design, leadership skills, coding, and how to network. I thought about some of my strengths and what I could offer to these girls, and finally I said, "I want to show girls how to run a successful business, so I'm going to teach a Financing 101 class." Learning how to manage money is important in life. Learning how to manage large amounts of money is critical in business. But I also wanted to focus on the role of being a female in the business world, so I thought about it some more and changed my response: "Actually, I'm going to do a Financing 101 course *specifically for girls.*"

I wasn't sure exactly what I meant by that. I knew that in my time as a business leader, I had been underestimated as a girl. But what was I going to talk about, and how was a Financing 101 course just for girls different from a Financing 101 class for everyone? I didn't know yet, but it was a good opportunity to think about it, write it down, and come up with a workshop about it. With my dad's help, and with guidance from a professor at the University of Texas, Austin, I came up with an interactive workshop that, to this day, I still use a version of when I talk about financing for girl business leaders. I called it my F.I.T.S. Plan. It was an easy way to help people think about how to generate a successful business idea while also focusing on basic financing skills. F.I.T.S. stands for Fix, Interest, Trends, Skills. It's a good acronym to remind anyone who wants to start a business of what idea *fits* for them. It was different from other workshops and lectures I'd been presenting about my company and bee conservation, and it allowed me to focus more on my role as a female entrepreneur and mentor for girls.

Being a teenage girl has its advantages and disadvantages. One of the main advantages I saw as a female entrepreneur was that 60 percent of my targeted consumers were female. A majority of those had children. In that way, I had a natural connection with buyers of my product. Another advantage of my age and gender was that I could engage with an entirely new and emerging group of young business leaders. In that sense, our conversations were always positive and encouraging. There is no denying there are a lot of disadvantages to being a teenage girl entrepreneur, but maybe the greatest disadvantage was that sometimes I doubted my own ability to do things—I thought they could only be accomplished by adults. I have learned, and am still learning, that with knowledge comes power at any age.

I'd never been out of the country before, and now I was going to travel nine thousand miles across the world to South Africa. I got my own passport, which was the greatest feeling in the world, and I had to learn how to pack. It sounds silly, but packing for a quick business trip was easy, but knowing how to pack for a longer international trip was its own skill set. Probably the worst part was all the vaccinations I needed—I hated getting shots!

After a long plane trip, we landed in the very welcoming city of Cape Town. My mom, who was always working on sharing my brand and story wherever we went, had arranged for a radio interview. So the first thing we did when we landed was visit the studios of WBBB radio. People at the station were so nice and connected us with other people who showed us around the city afterward.

I didn't realize it until I got there, but South Africa has the world's youngest population. There were young people everywhere, and South African leaders had been taking steps to make sure young women had just as many

opportunities as men to start success-ful businesses. My parents explained to me that in some countries in Africa, legal requirements had been made for governments to set aside a certain amount of money to support enterprises owned by women, youth, and the disabled.

Buzziness IDEA

Learning how to manage money is important in life. Learning how to manage large amounts of money is critical in business.

The summit took place at the Westin Hotel, in one of its large con-vention halls. As I sat at the hotel's fancy restaurant eating a large plate of fresh fruit, I read through the catalog of events and the businesses and backgrounds of these women entrepre-neurs. Not only was I thrilled and honored to be partic-ipating, but I realized I had not only been advocating for the bees, but I had been advocating for women entrepre-neurship along with these women just by going out there and starting a company. More and more women are start-ing businesses each year. It's reported that in the past two decades, the number of women-owned companies has increased by 114 percent. And yet many of us struggle to get funding for our businesses. I was determined to see that change. I would start with one lecture now, but a whole movement of new young entrepreneur girls was on the rise—I was determined to connect with some of them.

The main speaker of that year's summit was Jane Wurwand, the founder of Dermalogica, a skin care

product line. She started her company with a beauty school diploma, $14,000, and no investors. She had never taken a business course, nor was she a chemist. She started her career sweeping hair from the floor of a beauty salon. But through hard work, passion, and a tribe of loyal follow-ers, she explained to a packed conference hall, her brand grew in popularity. And she never gave up. She finished her keynote speech by saying, "The conversations you are destined to have here that will have the greatest impact will most likely be with a person you don't already know." That stuck with me. That was one of the greatest things about being an entrepreneur: meeting passionate people with ideas and not being afraid to reach out to each other. There were many great speakers, and I enjoyed everything about my trip to Cape Town, including teaching young girls about finance, meeting local South Africans, and, of course, going on a safari trip afterward.

My lecture took place in a room with about twenty other girls around my age. My mom, dad, and Jacob assisted me in my talk. Jacob passed out papers and took photographs, and my mom and dad helped the girls with the different exercises as I went through my lesson plan. It felt like an opportunity of a lifetime—to be in South Africa and working with these students—and we made it a family affair.

Buzziness
IDEA

One of the greatest things about being an entrepreneur is meeting passionate people with original ideas.

All of them were eager to hear my story about the bees and begin learning how to start and run their own successful companies. First, I introduced myself. I told them about my hobbies and where I live and what Austin is like. Then I told them about the two bee stings and why it's important to save the bees. I also shared with them about the growth of my company.

Then we focused on my new F.I.T.S. workshop. First, I asked each one of them if they had an idea of what they wanted to sell. Some of them did. As I've said earlier in this book, before you can start growing your business, you need the right idea, which is often the hardest part. I told them how lemonade was not my first idea, that painting colorful rocks to sell was. They laughed. Then we got to thinking about some ideas—good and bad.

HERE WERE THE STEPS OF MY F.I.T.S. WORKSHOP:

 FIX. This is when you see problems and think about ways to solve them. They can be large problems, like tackling poverty, hunger, or fresh water, or even the smallest ones, like not being able to easily open pickle jars. This step is critical because a lot of the problems that you face, others face, too, and a product or service that fixes is bound to be in demand. Many people who started a company based on fixing or solving something are social entrepreneurs like me: people who start a business with the aim of solving problems in the world.

INTERESTS. This is when you turn a hobby or passion into a company. Many people don't know that what they enjoy making or doing in their free time can be a way to earn money, whether it be baking or jewelry making. Each person has a unique way of doing these hobbies, so every product has a twist. One great thing about founding a company out of your interest is that it comes from passion, and the more passionate you are about what you do, the more fun you'll have while doing it—which in turn keeps you interested and the company growing.

TRENDS. This is a high-demand product that puts a twist to a craze or growing trend. All you have to do is look around for products that you see friends or family purchasing and make a change or improve it. For example, one kid entrepreneur I met saw how fidget spinners were such a craze and decided to start selling candy fidget spinners. Brilliant! Two great ideas in one. By doing this, he created a product but also knew people would buy it because it was already popular.

SKILLS. Do something that you are good at or have been practicing for some time. It could

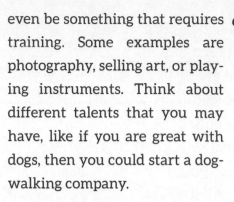

Buzziness
IDEA

As you brainstorm, be aware of the goals of your idea, its target market, what makes your idea unique, where you would sell your product, and whether you need a team.

even be something that requires training. Some examples are photography, selling art, or playing instruments. Think about different talents that you may have, like if you are great with dogs, then you could start a dog-walking company.

Once we had gone through the F.I.T.S. plan, we got started as a group creating a list of ideas, and other ideas began popping into their heads. This happens often in brainstorming sessions, which you'll do a lot of as an entrepreneur: one idea gives way to another. "Keep a journal attached to your body at all times," I said. As you are brainstorming, you should also be aware of the goals of your idea, its target market, what makes your idea unique, where you would sell your product, and whether you need a team. All the things that I had to think through as my business grew. I went on to talk about one of the most important things in business once you have an idea: creating a budget around that idea. And then marketing your business.

Then I told them the story of how when I was a little kid and just starting my company, I wanted the same doll my cousin had and that it would cost me $30. But my parents said I had to buy it with my own money. I didn't have

$30. That's when I earned $120 at a business fair and made enough to donate to an organization that helped save the bees *and* buy the doll. At the time, I was selling lemonade and giving to the bees, but I was also growing a business and becoming a social entrepreneur. By the time I was presenting this in South Africa, I realized I was also doing something else that was very important: I was becoming independent. Not just independent as a female entrepreneur but financially independent. I told the girls in the classroom to imagine what it would feel like to buy some things they wanted in life. That they wouldn't need to ask their parents or friends for help. They could buy it on their own. They all smiled.

"Being an entrepreneur and running a business takes a lot of hard work," I told them. "But success offers certain freedoms. In childhood we rely on our parents. Now think about how you want to be living five or ten years from now. Imagine your future. What do you want it to look like?" They wrote down their goals. They all in one way or another imagined themselves as financially independent working women, and that idea appealed to all of them.

Next, I talked about finding your voice as a female business leader. There are three prongs to this. First, you must find your own unique voice—the words you wish to use, the message you want to send to the world, the language you decide that others will be able to understand. Second, you need to speak with confidence so that you can communicate with all kinds of people comfortably—individually, in

Buzziness IDEA

Find your own unique voice. Speak with confidence, be fearless, encourage others, and be informed.

crowds, at a podium, doing demos, to the president of the United States, and when you become a keynote speaker at summits like this one. That voice is your fearless voice. Once you have found your words and your own fearless voice, then you can share your story and encourage other kid entrepreneurs to reach for their dreams. Finally, you need an informed voice to represent your company and speak up for it when necessary, when, let's say, there are legal or financial issues.

Then I talked about why I believe having a solid idea, being fearless, and finding your voice is so important for girls. I explained to them that for me, as an African American teenager in the business world, my voice could have easily been muffled. Even though black women entrepreneurs are the fastest-growing group of business owners in the United States, we still only get less than one percent of all venture funding for our companies. Because it is still an uphill battle for women, and girls in particular, we need to not only tell our stories but support each other's stories. We can do this on social media; we can specifically ask communities to carry more products by women entrepreneurs. Once they are on the shelves, we can buy those products, then encourage others to buy them as well. And we can ask others to support our products, too. We lead as a team.

A few weeks after my trip to South Africa, I was back in Austin sitting in the car at a red light with my mom when something occurred to me. It was evening time. Near my home there is the Texas School for the Deaf. The car next to us had the interior lights on, and one person was communicating to the other in sign language. The interior lights needed to be on so they could see each other speak. Without the light, it would be difficult to understand one another. It's not uncommon in our area to see people with their interior lights on at night speaking to each other in sign language. It occurred to me that one of the main problems CEOs talk a lot about is trying to find different ways to communicate with diverse groups of people so they understand. I got to thinking that I had discovered how to communicate on behalf of the bees in a way that made people want to listen. Sometimes you just need to turn the light on. You can't run a business in the dark. People are unable to hear your message. And sometimes the best way to communicate with others is to speak honestly and powerfully for those who need your help being heard.

CHAPTER FOURTEEN

Bee Important

One question I was always asked is, *How are the bees doing?* I wanted to tell people that over the years enough awareness had been raised and enough things had been done to help save them, but that wasn't true. In fact, US beekeepers reported in 2018 they lost nearly 40 percent of their honey bee colonies over the last few winters. The US Fish and Wildlife Service listed the rusty-patched bumblebee on the endangered species list in 2016. Rusty-patched bumblebees were once everywhere. Over the last decade, their population has decreased by almost 90 percent. That same year, my company saw a large increase in sales, and we were growing. But something seemed off. I didn't want to lose sight of the bees as my business got bigger. It could have been easy to set my mission aside while everything else was going on, but I couldn't and I wouldn't. In fact, I felt even more determined to protect the bees. So how could I stay true to our littlest pollinators beyond the business?

I was looking to effect more change as a social entrepreneur. My family and I brainstormed ideas. We could create some sort of app or a website that would log and inform others about bee research and bee-giving opportunities. But those, again, seemed like small steps.

After many conversations with my parents, I decided I wanted to start a nonprofit organization for the bees. But I had no idea how, and I wasn't sure I would have the time it took to run a not-for-profit business—even if I knew how to create and run one. Then one day—I was still twelve years old at the time—after a presentation I was giving about how to grow a business and save the bees, a man named Marc Pollick approached me. He had a really fun personality and was enthusiastic about helping me save the bees. Marc was the founder and president of the Giving Back Fund, which helps celebrities, athletes, and entrepreneurs start foundations and direct their funding toward things that would help make the greatest impact with their donations to their cause. The Giving Back Fund was unique in that it provided a quick way for a company to obtain a nonprofit status—called a 501(c)(3). Marc and his team would manage all the paperwork and tax documents, which would allow entrepreneurs like me to focus on raising funds and making a difference.

In my case, I wanted to start a nonprofit with a focus

Buzziness
<u>IDEA</u>

When you feel like you want to spend more time on the cause or mission associated with your business, there are many ways to create a nonprofit.

on educating people about the importance of bees, and through the proceeds of my lemonade donate healthy hives to the right organizations. It was a cause that I cared about, and I knew it needed a voice and a strategy separate from my lemonade business. It also felt like a good time in the business to focus more on social entrepreneurship and the bees because my business finally had a clear business plan in place and a strong team behind it. We were still in regular contact with Daymond John, who continued to help us with distribution and connecting us with buyers, and growth was strong and steady.

Now was as good a time as any, so I reached out to the Giving Back Fund to learn more. With Marc's help, I came up with my mission for my nonprofit, my goals, a list of what projects I wanted to work on, organizations I wanted to support, and a plan to put it in place. I founded the Healthy Hive Foundation in 2016.

The mission of the Healthy Hive Foundation is to increase honey bee awareness and the number of safe environments for bees to survive and thrive, through research, education, and preservation. With an established foundation, I wanted to turn my attention to funding important honey bee research: specifically why they are dying, what technology we can utilize to save them, how best we can protect and grow their habitats, and what alternatives to pesticides are available. I also wanted to travel the country and the world to teach other kids about how we can save the bees and why we need to

Healthy Hive
FOUNDATION

save them. Finally, I wanted to figure out how to get more funding toward my nonprofit, not just through the sales of my lemonade, but through fund-raisers and donors.

Here is what I was learning through this experience, and here is my advice to you: When you reach a point of feeling like you want to spend more time on the cause or mission associated with your business, there are many ways to create a separate entity. Starting a nonprofit has been rewarding, but it's a lot of work. It doesn't have to necessarily be a nonprofit; it can be an alternative with far less effort and cost. An easier path might just be to create a separate part of your organization dedicated solely to the good deeds of your mission. You could create an online donation page on your website. You could sponsor a local chapter of a national nonprofit that supports your cause. You, along with family and friends, could create a giving circle to raise money and communicate your mission's purpose. You could also start peer-to-peer fund-raisers at school and help distribute donations to various organizations.

But I had chosen the route of the nonprofit world, and I was ready to dive in. As I got comfortable learning the basics of running a foundation—I'm still very much in the learning phase—I began to enjoy the different sets of skills it offered me, particularly how to fund-raise. It also opened my eyes to an entirely different world of business. The nonprofit sector felt a little less competitive than the for-profit sector. There was less emphasis on profit gains and losses and more emphasis on social good and on my mission to protect the bees, which I loved. But it was also demanding in other ways—I would be asked about and would need to seek more opportunities for public speaking and fund-raising. I was so grateful the Giving Back Fund took care of all my paperwork and tax documents.

My first big fund-raiser was in Dallas, Texas. I was asked to speak at a golf fund-raiser. The agreement was, I would speak at the event about my story and my mission to save the bees as well as provide words of encouragement to the audience, and the fund-raiser would then make a donation to my Healthy Hive Foundation.

Fund-raising added a little bit more stress to my life, because seventh grade was already a lot of work. I had more homework and more tests, and I would need to be organized in order to balance everything. Like many seventh graders, I was taking practice high school placement tests. I also had volleyball practice every day after school and games on weekends. That year, in 2016, our team was undefeated, and we went to the playoffs. I wanted to be a part of it. But I saw my role as a bee advocate growing at the same intensity, and I didn't want to miss any opportunity to share and shape the conversation around saving the bees either. Plus, I felt a deeper commitment toward education than ever, and I wanted to make it one of my top priorities. I made sure I had an organized schedule so that I could balance all my roles as student, athlete, business owner, and philanthropist.

As I engaged with more people, businesses, and other nonprofits on behalf of my Healthy Hive Foundation, I was so proud to add the title of philanthropist to my many roles. I discovered most other bee nonprofits I was working with and donating toward focused only on honey bees—which is a great cause! And it made sense. Honey bees make the honey we eat. But there are twenty thousand species of bees in the world, and less than 5 percent of bees are the kind that makes honey. I was curious to learn more and support the less-talked-about solitary bees. Solitary bees don't produce honey, but they do pollinate plants—in fact, they may pollinate more than honey bees, which makes them critical for our food chain. I kept doing research. I felt strongly that it was important to bring awareness to all bees—solitary and honey. Then I came to think that maybe conversations would start with the bees but also include discussions around ecosystems and animal endangerment. It meant meeting with different organizations, such as environmental nonprofits separate from the beverage industry, and then sharing the information I'd gathered with sometimes small groups of individuals at churches or schools and sometimes larger groups, like golf fund-raisers, who were willing to donate through the

Healthy Hive Foundation. Large or small, I would encourage everyone I met to get to know the bees, take apiary and bee-keeping classes, plant a wildflower garden, find alternatives to using pesticides, pay attention to our littlest pollinators in yards and rooftop gardens, and protect them.

Entrepreneurs talk about "networking," and I was doing this with my foundation in different ways than I was when selling lemonade. I didn't have an elevator pitch when I talked about saving the bees; I had a clearly defined social good statement: *Through research, education, and preservation, the Healthy Hive Foundation is dedicated to increasing bee awareness and the number of safe environments for bees to survive and thrive.* Locally I met with groups in Austin doing incredible nonprofit work. I immediately joined with the Sustainable Food Center here in Austin. At the center I helped sponsor the addition of an apiary to their teaching garden. Schoolchildren can come and learn about the power of bees in our food chain and see their beehives in action. They meet with beekeepers and learn how honey is made.

Then other nonprofits with broader scope began to approach me to partner. I became a biodiversity ambassador for the National Park Foundation in 2016. For the national parks, I would do events in the field where we encouraged people to explore the outdoors and learn about our nation's parks and our environment. I also traveled to various parts of the country conducting scientific field experiments to study and teach students about our environment to include the impact of chemicals on crops and our pollinators.

I studied the effects of neonicotinoid pesticides on the bees. These types of pesticides are the worst for bees because the neonicotinic residue on treated plants collects in the pollen and the nectar. When bees land on a treated plant, the insecticide attacks the bee's nervous system, resulting in almost certain death. Scientists are still trying to determine how certain chemicals enter the bees' systems. They think pesticides get into the brain, which confuses them, and then they can't always find their way back to the hive. They also believe it could be that the bees who do return to the hive are feeding their hive the pesticides, and the whole colony gets poisoned and dies.

I learned more about the effects of land development and electromagnetic pollution on bees. This kind of research was so different from the research I had been doing online and at the library. I was experiencing the habitats of bees up close and personal—more importantly, I was witnessing their devastation. Entire colonies would succumb to the infamous Varroa mite and other parasites and viruses. Poor diet due to lack of flowers made entire hives sluggish and disinterested in mating.

Most people don't have time to stop their lives to do field research on various causes, but I did and would bring the field research data about the bees to people. If I heard there was a bee or honey festival, I would travel to it and talk to people about various topics related to bees. At one event, they crowned a girl a Honey Bee Queen! She became an ambassador for the bees. People were doing incredible things everywhere. I felt like not only was I witnessing a movement as I saw messages to save the bees spread, but I was part of that movement.

In early 2018, the European Union put in place a ban on the use of neonicotinoids; Canada was in heavy discussions to do the same. Small communities in the United States were getting in on the action and banning pesticide use. I saw my work and the work of many bee advocates putting pressure on certain industries and making a difference. But was it a real difference?

In 2019, the US Environmental Protection Agency (EPA) announced a ban on twelve of the neonicotinoid pesticides being produced by three large chemical companies. Seven out of the twelve pesticides had been used on corn, soybeans, and many other fruit, nut, and vegetable crops. This seemed like a huge win for the bees, and progress was definitely being made. But there is way more that could be done. There are still almost fifty other types of neonicotinoid pesticides being used. Reducing the amount of pesticides is a step in the right direction.

But a bigger step would be to change the agricultural industry's current way of thinking and current farming practices and return to sustainable farming. Traditional actions can restore bee populations. We could work toward 100 percent organic farming practices. That would definitely help bees return to their natural pollinating ways and renew their populations.

HOW TO SAVE THE BEES

1   **BE INFORMED.** Read and share as much as you can about bees and other pollinators!

2   **BUY LOCAL HONEY.** The backyard bee-keeping movement is here to stay! Support local beekeepers by shopping local.

3   **MIX IT UP.** Plant bee-friendly flowers with different colors, shapes, and bloom times.

4   **DON'T SPRAY IT!** Avoid using herbi-cides or pesticides in the garden. Ladybugs, spiders, and praying mantises will naturally keep pest populations in check.

5   **BE A SWEET FRIEND.** Did you know that I donate money from the sale of my lemonade to organizations fighting hard to save the bees?

6   **SHARE THE BUZZ.** Share my facts, sto-ries, and videos. Social media is an awesome way to raise awareness and spread information on saving the bees!

I continued to share recent findings and results with others. My workshops had changed from my early days of the trifold poster and cutout photos I'd found on the internet of "bee facts" to a much more detailed PowerPoint presentation and a video of specific research being done and data collected. As I learned new statistics, I included newer and more information.

Sometimes I would participate in events and conferences as a social entrepreneur talking about saving the bees, and sometimes I would participate as Mikaila Ulmer, the CEO of Me & the Bees. It wasn't out of the ordinary to be at a business conference like Natural Products Expo West presenting a talk titled "When Life Gives You Lemons: Brand Equity and Storytelling" and the next week be at an elementary school talking about "Dreaming like a Kid" and ways to save the bees.

I never knew exactly how many people would be at certain events and what kinds of conversations we would be having. There were business events where we would end up talking about saving bees and social good events where we would end up talking about business.

I loved presenting information and interacting with the audience, but not every event went smoothly. Sometimes I mixed up my words, other times I forgot to include whole pieces of information that I wanted to talk about. One time, I hosted an event sponsored by an organization. The event took place in an auditorium. Usually I get more excited than nervous about these events, but for some reason, that day I was really nervous. Maybe it was because when I looked out at the crowd before getting on stage, there were not a lot of people there, and the auditorium was huge. I wasn't wearing my bee costume anymore, but I did try to wear my signature yellow. I looked out from behind the curtain and told my mom, "It's almost empty out there!" The people who sponsored the event were upset as well, and I wasn't sure how I felt presenting to an almost-empty large room.

But my mom put things into perspective: "The people who did show up are here to learn how to save the bees. That's more people than the day before, isn't it?" She also said that no matter how large or small the audience was, I had to give it 100 percent. It was true. It didn't matter the size of the audience—people were learning and engaging, and I had to share all that I had learned.

Afterward a girl approached me and said, "I saw you on *Shark Tank*. I liked you so much. It got me interested in wanting to save the bees, too."

Those were *the moments!* It was all about those moments. Those people. That girl. And the bees. When I have a challenging day, or I think no one else cares, if I know I saved a bee or inspired someone else to save a bee or start their own cause, then I know I've made a difference.

I realized even if it was just a few people, those few people would teach other people about the importance of saving the bees. And other people will tell more people. And so on. And that's how a movement gets its wings.

"Even one person can make a difference," my mother reminded me.

Even one person can make a difference.

President Obama's senior advisor Valerie Jarrett once said, "Power doesn't come from the top down—it comes from the bottom up." I've thought a lot about that statement. Power doesn't necessarily come from those with the most influence and the most money. Sometimes power comes from little movements, or even one individual with a lot of passion. I had the power to save the bees. No one was stopping me, so I figured I might as well keep going.

As I gained confidence in the nonprofit world, I found more ways to collaborate with other causes. For example, on World Water Day, I sent dozens of boxes of lemonade on behalf of Me & the Bees to Flint, Michigan, where citizens had been drinking the city's contaminated drinking water for years. My message was one of support. I didn't just need to support the bees; I could use my mission to help support other people and other organizations fighting different causes, too.

I have received many awards for my activism and nonprofit work, along with my role as a young, female entrepreneur. I was humbled and honored to receive such awards as the Texas Entrepreneur Award, GrassROOTS Community Foundation Award, the Tribeca Disruptive Innovation Award, the *Ebony* Power 100 list of Future Achievers, along with many others. In October 2016, I was humbled to receive the Eleanor Roosevelt Val-Kill Medal for "significant contributions to humanitarian efforts" in my community. At age twelve, I was the youngest person to ever receive the award. A few past recipients included Hillary Clinton, James Earl Jones, Harry Belafonte, Christopher Reeve, Queen Noor of Jordan, and Gloria Steinem!

Once I started really thinking about my business and my mission, my lemonade company became a social good endeavor first, and the profit followed. I thought about why I set up my very first lemonade stand: *Buy a cup. Save a bee.* My story about the bee stings and the lemonade stand was evolving before my eyes. I was no longer that little girl in a bee costume selling lemonade in my front yard for a dollar. I was a social entrepreneur, and I was also an award-winning activist whose mission it was to save the bees through making lemonade. And it felt just right.

CHAPTER FIFTEEN

From the Bee Suite to the C-Suite

We rise by lifting others.

—ROBERT INGERSOLL

A term you will often hear in business is "C-Suite." The *C* stands for "Chief," as in positions like Chief Executive Officer (CEO), Chief Operating Officer (COO), and Chief Financial Officer (CFO). So C-Suite means the highest position in a company. Early on, I knew I was different from most CEOs running businesses—most CEOs hadn't started their careers in kindergarten. I always joked it was a great way to get people's attention. But it wasn't just my age, and it wasn't just being passionate about saving the bees, it was that I *started* with my passion and mission first, over profit.

It was this mission-first business mind-set that opened doors and gave me opportunities to meet with other CEOs doing social good work. Many of those leaders offered great advice, which I would write down from time to time: "Success isn't happiness, but happiness is the key to success." Or "Be the person in the room who has the solution, not the problem." Or, I liked this one: "Start young so that you can focus on your mission in the future." I had been given lots of advice from leaders and influencers since I started

Buzziness IDEA

No matter what age you are, you can see your company as a vision-driven social good machine, not just a company that makes a product and turns a profit.

Me & the Bees. The advice I gave back to them was simple: No matter what age you are, you can see your company as vision-driven social good machine, not just a company that makes a product and turns a profit. *Give before you get.* It's that simple. I heard it growing up from my own grandfather, I heard the message repeated at church, and I say it to other business owners now.

By 2017, my bottles of lemonade were in over seven hundred stores coast-to-coast. We'd more than doubled that store count number by 2019. As I grew in my role as CEO, social entrepreneur, bee ambassador, and philanthropist, I learned another useful business lesson: I could use my platform to get the message of my mission out about the bees.

Buzziness IDEA

The most successful companies are run by founders who truly love what they do and are passionate about their product and purpose.

I had an opportunity to do just that when I spoke at WE Day Seattle in 2016. WE Day is a youth empowerment event where thousands of students come together to celebrate working together for global causes. Right before I got onstage, I met Satya Nadella, who is the CEO of Microsoft. I was so honored to meet him! Then I found out *he* was the one who would be introducing me and my mission to save the bees in front of sixteen thousand people! It was a very big moment.

My message to the audience was clear: The most successful companies are run by founders who truly love what they do and are passionate about their product and purpose. Find something you love to do. And always, *always* give back to your community.

After the event, Mr. Nadella and I promised to stay in touch. And we did stay in touch. A lot. Over time, Me & the Bees partnered with Microsoft—they helped provide my business with office products and a database and tech support to help run my company more smoothly. I also became one of Microsoft's "people who inspire." For them, they see a kid entrepreneur reaching a whole new customer base of Generation Z buyers and future buyers. For me, they've helped improve my business and introduced

With Chris Capossela

With Satya Nadella

me to new trends and technology, which in turn allows me to help spread the message of the bees. When I told them I wanted to learn more about what research was being done to save the bees, they flew me out to meet with their Chief Marketing Officer (CMO), Chris Capossela.

After getting to know them for a while, I was brought on a tour of the famed Building 99, where Microsoft does research on new technologies. I got to see some of the designs and innovations they were working on, including their work on bee research! I saw how they'd created micro-scopic transistors to put on bees that track their movement. By tracking bees, they can collect critical data such as the activity happening in their hives and how bees react to

certain environmental conditions, like extreme tempera-
ture changes and air and noise pollution.

After my visit, I returned home with a greater under-
standing of the science and research behind my cause. But
how could I reach new customers and educate more people?
Reaching new customers is always a goal of any business
leader. Finding new channels and new ways of introducing
your product is a challenge for everyone in any industry. I
would need to keep working. This was in spring 2017.

In July 2017, we got important news. After our success
on *Shark Tank*, and with the help of Daymond John, we
had been actively talking with other potential investors
who might be able to help grow our business even more.
The process of meeting with potential investors and getting them to commit funding can be slow and oftentimes
discouraging. But then one day, we got the news that we
had officially received funding from a group of pretty cool
investors thanks to an amazing man, Mr. Humble, who
also invested in me. He brought together former and current NFL players Arian Foster, Glover Quin, Duane Brown,
Jonathan Grimes, Omar Bolden, Bobby Wagner, Darius
Slay, Sherrick McManis, EJ Manuel, and Malik Jackson for
a combined $810,000, and in 2019, they invested $750,000
more. As *Fast Company* notes—via Renae Bluitt, director of
2019 Netflix documentary *She Did That*—of the $100 billion

in venture funding that goes to American entrepreneurs, less than 3 percent goes to women, and only 0.02 percent goes to black women. So, for me, an African American female teen entrepreneur, to get more than $1.5 million from this group of individual investors was astonishing.

Funding like this is critical for any company's growth. Start-ups like mine are always seeking investors. Getting that kind of money would allow Me & the Bees to grow in ways we could have never imagined. As a company, we had expanded to different regions of the United States, but we were still struggling to fill orders and produce enough runs. The funding provided by this group of NFL players would give us the money we needed to make larger production runs. With an increase in production, we would be able to further build a pipeline. We would also be able to expand our sales force.

With significant financial backing and a product that was now being sold in over one thousand stores, I now felt like I had a legitimate "seat at the table," and in 2018, I found myself on the top floor of Coca-Cola's headquarters in Atlanta.

By that point, I had gotten used to being the youngest person in the room and, besides my mother, sometimes the only female. But I wasn't used to being in a room of top beverage industry experts. The topic of conversation? Sugar. How would our industry move forward and reduce the amount of sugar in our products? At the event, I heard some of the great beverage icons of our age talking about the future of beverages, the rapidly evolving industry, how small companies can compete with larger companies, and how not to follow current trends but see into the future by five to ten years.

Honest Tea co-founder Seth Goldman hosted a fireside chat afterward and answered questions that were talked about earlier in the day. Seth Goldman knew a lot about being a small fish in a world of big beverage companies. In 1998, he had started with an idea for a delicious organic iced tea without the sugar. His iced tea took off, and eventually he sold his company to Coca-Cola. Before Coke acquired his company, his bottles were in fifteen thousand locations. After they bought his company, they were in over one hundred thousand.

I wanted to hear his story and everything he learned along the way. I told him I had created an organic lemonade using honey and flaxseed. He was immediately interested. Growth is important for a bee colony's survival. Growth is also important for a company's survival. For my company, growth wasn't just about lemonade or the bees, but about the honey that the bees made and supporting the local bee-keepers that supplied us with the honey. And growth was also in the lemons that the bees pollinated and the number of crates of lemons I ordered to create my lemonade. The bees were in every sip of my juice.

I would often think about how a bee colony grew and functioned when I thought about how my business grew and functioned. How does a bee colony grow? (To be sure, there are lots of different kinds of beehives.) Honey bee colonies grow gradually as their hives grow. They have bees dedicated to very specific tasks. Successful businesses are like successful beehives. Worker bees work to make the wax, which is used to form the cells for honey storage. They communicate through dancing. When a bee finds a good crop to feed from, they'll return to the hive and do what's called a waggle dance to guide other bees in the direction of the food.

I often imagined what more business leaders would look like if they grooved a little more. Maybe I wouldn't be able to compete with large corporations (just yet!), but perhaps they'd learn a little something from my waggle.

CHAPTER SIXTEEN

A Decade with Me & the Bees

I pinch myself thinking about what came of two bee stings in a ten-year span. Building a company from the ground up is not a sprint, it's a marathon; it takes a lot of time and patience, a lot of failure and successes, a lot of knocking on doors, phone calls, and taking risks before a company hits its stride. My business's success didn't happen overnight. It took years. It will take more years.

According to the Small Business Administration, about two-thirds of companies survive two years in business, half of all businesses will survive five years, and only one-third will survive ten years. My advice is to stay committed to your vision and mission and *don't give up!* If you continue to invest time and energy into a cause you're passionate about, you will get there. Some days might be more difficult than others. But looking back on a decade of hard work, it's worth the effort.

So far, the save-the-bees message on my bottled lemonade has reached over 1,500 stores across America, with a total output of 1.3 million bottles. Now, with more time dedicated to outreach, I have over eighty thousand followers on social media. I share the latest in bee research and conservation with them on a regular basis. I was honored to be named by *Time* magazine as one of the thirty most influential teens in America, which means I have been good at sharing information and educating others.

Many people have asked me what's next for Me & the Bees as we celebrate "Ten Years in Buzziness."

First, with the help of added funding from the NFL investors and as a result of steady growth and loyal customers, I was able to reduce the cost of my bottled lemonade to a shelf

Buzziness
IDEA

Stay committed to your vision and mission and don't give up! If you continue to invest time and energy into a cause you're passionate about, you will get there.

Cheers to
10 YEARS
------ OF ------
beelieving!

price of $2.99 for a 12-ounce bottle. That felt great! Second, customers were looking for ways to cut sugar out of their beverage consumption, so Me & the Bees got back to work and hired a food scientist to help us find a way to reduce sugar. We ended up adding even more monk fruit extract— which does not raise blood sugar levels—and were able to cut the sugar from our lemonade by 25 percent with up to 33 percent fewer calories without altering the flavor.

These two things, reducing the cost and lowering the amount of sugar, had been long-term goals of mine. But there were other things I wanted to do with my lemonade product going forward. I was exploring new flavors, a sparkling drink version, maybe Popsicles, and the idea of bottling juice in gallon sizes. I was also looking into lighter packaging. I was always thinking of new ways to grow my product and my brand—why not skin care, or a line of perfumes?—and it's something you'll want to do as you grow your brand. *Always be thinking of what's next.*

Of course, then there's the bees. I plan to focus much more of my time on my Healthy Hive Foundation. Since education is one of the primary objectives of my foundation—because without an educated population, it is unlikely that pollinator protection will become a national priority—I am in the process of creating a weeklong pollinator education program.

The idea of the program is to run a short mixed-delivery pollinator educational program at schools from K through fifth grade. I will work with schools on STEM projects to teach kids about different aspects of bee conservation. The

curriculum will last a week, and it is set to have each day focus on a different part of the pollinator topic. Monday will begin with a general overview of pollinators. Tuesday will be a more detailed analysis of individual honey bees. Wednesday will be a general look into what overall life is like in a beehive. Thursday is a big-picture exploration of the threat that pollinators face today. And finally, Friday is an entrepreneurship workshop and lemonade social for all schools. A general rundown of bee week is shown in the illustration below.

Bee Week Lesson Plans

Monday	Tuesday	Wednesday	Thursday	Friday
The Basics	Traits of Honey Bees	Life in the Hive	Honey Bees and Their Environment	Entrepreneurs

Outcomes will be not only to educate students but to inspire them to become passionate about bee conservation.

My goal is to fully develop this program and to bring my bee curriculum to low-income schools first. Because what I've learned is that even though millions of dollars per year are poured into teaching environmental studies in the classroom, too many schools in low-income areas do not have access to good programs. Most environmental programs in those areas are sidelined, and funding is instead diverted into professional development programs with a focus on test scores. There is still a lot of planning and fund-raising to be done before I'm ready to launch this program, but I've received lots of interest from schools already.

The Healthy Hive Foundation is now able to dedicate more of its resources to research as well. Recently we've partnered with San Francisco State University on a research project to better understand the impact of recent wildfires on honey bees. Because of climate change, California has had an unusual number of large wildfires over the last few years—particularly in Napa and Sonoma Counties in Northern California.

Healthy Hive is starting to work with these researchers to track how bee pollination changes following wildfires: What happens to their hives when they are impacted by fires, and how do bees find other resources to survive? The ultimate goal is to see if these big changes to their environment make bees more resilient or if they devastate whole colonies. I will be gathering and reporting on that data soon.

When I think about how many years of my life I've dedi-cated to the bees, how many beehives I have donated, how much my foundation will help educate others about the importance of bees, I feel good knowing I've made a dif-ference in this world. But there was something else I feel I have achieved over the last ten years by being a vocal kid entrepreneur. I hope and believe I have made it normal, or at least more within reach, for kids to create and grow their own businesses.

Being an entrepreneur, having an entrepreneurial mind-set, is a rewarding experience. You get to come up with an infinite number of ideas. Some ideas you'll never use. Some ideas you'll start on, and they'll fade away. But some ideas you'll have are really good ones. At the end of the day, being able to use creative ideas to help solve prob-lems is a great feeling. You'll also get to meet some amazing people along the way.

When I started my business, I used to dream of my lem-onade being in every neighborhood. Today I dream of being able to inspire every kid in every school district to become a social entrepreneur—to notice problems in the world and help fix them through business-minded solutions.

My generation, Generation Z, is a very social genera-tion. Probably more social than any other generation in history because of social media and our access to all kinds of technology. We have been born during a time when we have all these tools we can use to start a company—but also to start a movement.

There are many problems in this world, and many missions to have. So figure out what you need to do to solve a problem and reach out to others who are also concerned about the same thing. Use your youth, and all that has been created for us to our advantage, and build your hive.

When I first started helping the bees, that's all I thought I was doing. Their numbers were decreasing, and I wanted to change that. What I found out was I wasn't just saving the bees; I was protecting our food supply. Kids are the ones who will inherit tomorrow. We need to make sure what we're doing today is what's needed to ensure there *is* a tomorrow.

Here are some of the most important things I've learned over the last ten years:

- Keep your products simple. Keep them clean of additives and chemicals.
- Make real promises to people and keep them.
- Write thank-you letters.
- Support entrepreneurs, especially local ones.
- Invest in the future.
- Strive to do your best in everything you do. Win or lose, it's the input that matters.
- Our culture reinforces perfection through social media. Don't fall for it! Perfect is never to

be attained. It's okay to make mistakes and be messy every once in a while.

- If you decide to be a shark, like the kind on *Shark Tank*, be a responsible shark and choose to invest in businesses with a mission.
- If you get stung by a bee, don't be afraid of them, make lemonade.

This is the final lesson I will offer to you: Be a sweet business owner. You can be sweet, and you can be profitable in business. There's the stereotype that businesspeople are hungry and greedy for money. Let's retire that—and other stereotypes—for good! You can be successful, and you can make money, and you can still make an impact at the same time. So to everyone I say: Use your lemons and create your own kind of lemonade!

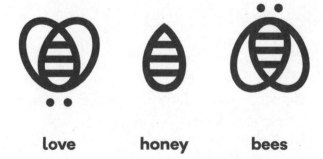

love   honey   bees

Acknowledgments

I would have

never imagined that I'd be running my own company one day—as a kid—let
alone writing a book about it! When I first started teaching
workshops about bees and my business, I was a bit nervous,
especially when the other kids were older than me. That's
when my parents reassured me with some words of wisdom I will never forget: "Everyone has something to learn,
and everyone has something to teach." Writing this book
and growing Me & the Bees have been about teaching and
sharing my story, but also about learning from others. *Bee
Fearless* is the result of the efforts of countless people who
all pitched in to help me paint a complete picture.

First, I'd like to thank all those who helped Me & the

Bees get to where it is today. I am so grateful for the support I have received from my family, fans, and "beelievers," including our customers, retailers, partners, and investors. This is more than I could have ever dreamed of—and I dream big.

I'd be crazy if I didn't give a million thanks to all those who made this book happen. It all started with my long phone calls with Ms. Brin, who basically became a member of our family for a couple of days! I also want to thank everyone who rallied to support me and my business, especially Ms. Alyssa Henkin, Andrea Wade, and Stacey Barney.

I want to send the deepest gratitude to my hive: my mentors, my muses, and all the "make-it-happeners." Huge thanks to my parents; my little brother, Jacob, a.k.a. our #1 sales rep; my older brother, Khalil; my grandparents; and "auntie" Sabreena Geddie, who made all those trips possible. I also couldn't have done it without one of our key advisors, Joe O'Hara, the creative gurus at Team One, and my incredible ops team, including Mr. Geoff. Last but not least, to my friends (you know who you are): Thanks for always having my back and beelieving in me!

Photo © 2020 by Jai Lennard

Mikaila Ulmer is the founder and CEO of Me & the Bees Lemonade. Using her great-granny Helen's flaxseed honey lemonade recipe, Mikaila launched her business from her home in Austin, Texas, in 2009. After landing a deal with Daymond John on *Shark Tank*, her lemonade is now sold in grocery stores across the country. In 2016, Mikaila launched her Healthy Hive Foundation, and 10 percent of the net profits from the sale of her lemonade goes to saving our honey bees.

Connect with Mikaila at
meandthebees.com
or on Facebook, Instagram, and Twitter
@MikailasBees

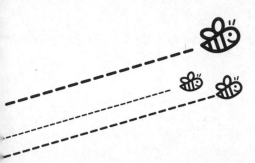

Brin Stevens is a professional ghostwriter and has collaborated with authors on a number of books. She lives in Newburyport, Massachusetts, with her husband and two daughters.